MODERNIZING EXPORT CONTROLS: PROTECTING CUTTING-EDGE TECHNOLOGY AND U.S. NATIONAL SECURITY

HEARING

BEFORE THE

COMMITTEE ON FOREIGN AFFAIRS HOUSE OF REPRESENTATIVES

ONE HUNDRED FIFTEENTH CONGRESS

SECOND SESSION

MARCH 14, 2018

Serial No. 115–116

Printed for the use of the Committee on Foreign Affairs

Available via the World Wide Web: http://www.foreignaffairs.house.gov/ or
http://www.gpo.gov/fdsys/

U.S. GOVERNMENT PUBLISHING OFFICE

29–363PDF   WASHINGTON : 2018

For sale by the Superintendent of Documents, U.S. Government Publishing Office
Internet: bookstore.gpo.gov   Phone: toll free (866) 512–1800; DC area (202) 512–1800
Fax: (202) 512–2104   Mail: Stop IDCC, Washington, DC 20402–0001

COMMITTEE ON FOREIGN AFFAIRS

EDWARD R. ROYCE, California, *Chairman*

CHRISTOPHER H. SMITH, New Jersey
ILEANA ROS-LEHTINEN, Florida
DANA ROHRABACHER, California
STEVE CHABOT, Ohio
JOE WILSON, South Carolina
MICHAEL T. McCAUL, Texas
TED POE, Texas
DARRELL E. ISSA, California
TOM MARINO, Pennsylvania
MO BROOKS, Alabama
PAUL COOK, California
SCOTT PERRY, Pennsylvania
RON DeSANTIS, Florida
MARK MEADOWS, North Carolina
TED S. YOHO, Florida
ADAM KINZINGER, Illinois
LEE M. ZELDIN, New York
DANIEL M. DONOVAN, JR., New York
F. JAMES SENSENBRENNER, JR.,
  Wisconsin
ANN WAGNER, Missouri
BRIAN J. MAST, Florida
FRANCIS ROONEY, Florida
BRIAN K. FITZPATRICK, Pennsylvania
THOMAS A. GARRETT, JR., Virginia
JOHN R. CURTIS, Utah

ELIOT L. ENGEL, New York
BRAD SHERMAN, California
GREGORY W. MEEKS, New York
ALBIO SIRES, New Jersey
GERALD E. CONNOLLY, Virginia
THEODORE E. DEUTCH, Florida
KAREN BASS, California
WILLIAM R. KEATING, Massachusetts
DAVID N. CICILLINE, Rhode Island
AMI BERA, California
LOIS FRANKEL, Florida
TULSI GABBARD, Hawaii
JOAQUIN CASTRO, Texas
ROBIN L. KELLY, Illinois
BRENDAN F. BOYLE, Pennsylvania
DINA TITUS, Nevada
NORMA J. TORRES, California
BRADLEY SCOTT SCHNEIDER, Illinois
THOMAS R. SUOZZI, New York
ADRIANO ESPAILLAT, New York
TED LIEU, California

AMY PORTER, *Chief of Staff*   THOMAS SHEEHY, *Staff Director*
JASON STEINBAUM, *Democratic Staff Director*

CONTENTS

Page

WITNESSES

The Honorable Mario Mancuso, partner, Kirkland and Ellis, LLP (former Undersecretary for Industry and Security, U.S. Department of Commerce) .. 3

The Honorable Alan Larson, senior international policy advisor, Covington and Burling, LLP (former Undersecretary for Economic, Business, and Agricultural Affairs, U.S. Department of State) 10

The Honorable Kevin Wolf, partner, Akin Gump Strauss Hauer and Feld, LLP (former Assistant Secretary for Export Administration, Bureau of Industry and Security, U.S. Department of Commerce) 17

LETTERS, STATEMENTS, ETC., SUBMITTED FOR THE HEARING

The Honorable Mario Mancuso: Prepared statement 6
The Honorable Alan Larson: Prepared statement 12
The Honorable Kevin Wolf: Prepared statement 19

APPENDIX

Hearing notice 50
Hearing minutes 51
The Honorable Gerald E. Connolly, a Representative in Congress from the Commonwealth of Virginia: Prepared statement 53
Written responses from the witnesses to questions submitted for the record by:
The Honorable Adam Kinzinger, a Representative in Congress from the State of Illinois 54
The Honorable Ann Wagner, a Representative in Congress from the State of Missouri 55

MODERNIZING EXPORT CONTROLS: PROTECTING CUTTING-EDGE TECHNOLOGY AND U.S. NATIONAL SECURITY

WEDNESDAY, MARCH 14, 2018

House of Representatives,
Committee on Foreign Affairs,
Washington, DC.

The committee met, pursuant to notice, at 10:00 a.m., in room 2172 Rayburn House Office Building, Hon. Edward Royce (chairman of the committee) presiding.

Chairman ROYCE. This committee will come to order. And today the committee is going to review our export controls and our foreign investment review process. Both are critical to protecting our national security and, of course, protecting our economic edge.

The United States, as we all know, is the world's largest exporter of goods and services, and our trade relationships as well as our leadership in science, engineering and manufacturing support between them tens of millions of good-paying American jobs.

Alarmingly, our competitive edge is increasingly under attack by policies from China and Russia and from others that seek to obtain advanced technologies and intellectual property by hook or by crook. As some may recall, in 2011 this committee held a hearing on China's "indigenous innovation" policy and at that time I noted the Chinese Government has been turning up the pressure on U.S. and other foreign business to share sensitive technology with Chinese state-owned enterprises as the cost of selling in the Chinese market. This is especially true today.

Making matters worse, our outdated regulatory safeguards have potential gaps. Those gaps could permit transfers to potential adversaries of the "know-how" essential to sensitive emerging technologies like artificial intelligence as well as robotics.

In this global economy, turning inward is not the solution to these challenges. But we also cannot allow others to cheat U.S. employers or, worse, use our sensitive technology to undermine our own national security.

And that's why Ranking Member Engel and I have introduced the Export Control Reform Act of 2018, which would repeal the expired Cold War era Export Administration Act of 1979. We would replace it with a modern statutory authority to regulate dual-use items. Under our approach, we would modernize U.S. export control laws and regulations and they will continue to have broad authority governing the transfer of less sensitive military and dual-use in technology to foreign persons whether that transfer takes place abroad or here in the United States.

As governments like Beijing and others pursue their hard-edge strategies to acquire advanced technologies from the U.S. and from our allies, our bill utilizes unilateral controls where necessary and it also will improve coordination with allies to strengthen export controls and inward investment security.

Meanwhile, the Committee on Foreign Investment in the United States—and that's CFIUS—would continue to review certain "covered transactions." Those are defined as the acquisition or control by foreign persons over a U.S. business. The vast majority of these investments are productive and should be welcomed.

Modernized U.S. export controls and appropriately crafted CFIUS reforms are complementary responses to the challenges we face. Together, they should improve the ability of the U.S. to remain a leader in innovation and to strengthen the industrial base and to protect the technologies essential to national security.

Our goal is an efficient regulatory system that promotes both our national security and our economic prosperity and we have with us today three practitioners in the field, each with long experience in the CFIUS process and with U.S. export controls, and we hope their testimony today will provide the committee with insights into how to proceed on these important and challenging issues.

And I will turn to the Democratic side in case we have any members who would like to make an opening statement, if they would. Otherwise, we will go to the witnesses.

Mr. SIRES. No, I don't have any statement. Thank you very much. Thank you for being here.

Chairman ROYCE. And so this morning the distinguished panel includes Mr. Mancuso. Mario is a partner at Kirkland & Ellis and previously he served as the Undersecretary of Commerce for Industry and Security, and as the Deputy Assistant Secretary of Defense for Special Operations and Combating Terrorism.

We have Ambassador Alan Larson. He serves as senior international policy advisor at Covington & Burling. Previously, Ambassador Larson served in a series of senior government positions including as the Undersecretary of State for Economic, Business, and Agricultural Affairs, and as the Ambassador for the Organization for Economic Cooperation and Development.

And we have Mr. Kevin Wolf, partner at Akin Gump Strauss Hauer & Feld. Previously, he served as the Assistant Secretary of Commerce for Export Administration within the Bureau of Industry and Security.

So without any objection, the witnesses' full prepared statements are going to be made part of the record and members here are going to have 5 calendar days to submit any statements or questions or any extraneous material for the record.

And we will begin with Mario Mancuso. And we will ask him to summarize, sir, your remarks and we will go down the panel.

STATEMENT OF THE HONORABLE MARIO MANCUSO, PARTNER, KIRKLAND AND ELLIS, LLP (FORMER UNDERSECRETARY FOR INDUSTRY AND SECURITY, U.S. DEPARTMENT OF COMMERCE)

Mr. MANCUSO. Thank you. Chairman Royce, Ranking Member Engel, and other distinguished members of the committee, thank you for the opportunity to testify this morning. I am delighted, obviously, to be with all of you and with my fellow panelists.

As Chairman Royce mentioned, my name is Mario Mancuso. Over the course of my career in government I've had the great privilege to serve in a variety of roles in the U.S. national security and foreign policy enterprise.

I served as Undersecretary for Industry and Security, as Deputy Assistant Secretary of Defense for Special Operations, a member of the Global Market Board at the National Intelligence Council, and as a forward-deployed military officer in combat.

In these roles, I learned a great deal about how U.S. national security is conceived, debated, and articulated in the interagency, how statecraft is actually operationalized and how U.S. national security is advanced on the ground.

I learned a great deal about the differences between ideas and execution, between inputs and outputs, the importance of legal authorities, resources, and accountability and the need for modesty, especially in presuming what we know and do not know and cannot know and do.

Today, I am a visiting senior fellow at the Hudson Institute for International Security where I continue to work on questions that relate to U.S. national security strategy and statecraft in the emerging security environment.

I am also a partner at Kirkland and Ellis where my practice focuses on matters that relate to U.S. national security regulation of international activities.

I want to be clear from the outset I am here today in my personal capacity. The views I express here are mine alone and they should not be construed as the views of Kirkland and Ellis or its clients.

I am here to offer some observations in my capacity as a former government official about these topics and to answer your questions.

I will not discuss any specific case or matter that has been or is current before the U.S. Government.

As this committee knows well, both CFIUS and export controls are important instruments of U.S. statecraft. By design, they aim to effectuate a selective denial strategy, which itself is premised on an important assumption—that the U.S. has certain things that others want and don't have.

While globalization has rendered that assumption outdated in many areas, for certain emerging and foundational technologies—for example, artificial intelligence, robotics, augmented and virtual reality, et cetera—that assumption is still generally true today.

On the other hand, while globalization has diminished our lead in certain technology areas, it has also been central to our economic and, by extension, our national security success.

One need only look at U.S. overmatch advantages in nuclear and electronics-enabled capabilities at critical junctures in our history to see how economic scale and technological superiority worked hand in hand in service of our global preeminence.

In this connection, as this committee considers the contribution of CFIUS and export controls to U.S. national security, I would invite the committee to keep in mind two questions which may help frame the discussion.

First, at this time in our history, what's the optimal balance for the U.S. to strike between economic openness and restrictiveness in order for our country to secure the most important advantages of openness while mitigating its greatest risks; second, whether in light of that equilibrium CFIUS and the current export control regime is by virtue of its resources and authorities properly configured to effectively implement and maintain this balance.

In the interests of facilitating this, I'll just offer some observations. I won't offer all of them. All of them will be in my written testimony, but just a few to start things off here.

First, foreign direct investment—FDI—is critical to U.S. economic vitality. The collective economic strength and vitality of our economy to which FDI clearly contributes helps resource our investment in national defense and extends our soft power reach around the world.

While the U.S. remains a preferred global destination for FDI, our global share of FDI has declined in recent years. Because of its many benefits, this should be concerning to U.S. policymakers including U.S. national security policymakers.

Indeed, nations today must compete for foreign direct investment. A failure to consistently attract benign FDI into the U.S. would present a long-term systemic national security risk to the United States.

But while FDI is generally good, certain transactions do in fact present transaction-specific national security risks. The policy question to consider, therefore, is not how to balance economic and national security interests but how to balance systemic and transaction specific national security risks.

In recent years, strategic competition between the U.S. and China has increased across multiple domains—economic, political, diplomatic, and military—and there is no reason to believe that that competition will abate in coming years.

China is actively pursuing a well-resourced coordinated science and technology strategy that seeks to bolster indigenous Chinese innovation and to position China to be the world's technology leader.

A number of pillars of this strategy, as Chairman Royce rightly pointed out, have been described in various official Chinese Government pronouncements such as "Made in China," a number of Five-Year Plans, and certain published technology roadmaps.

If successful in its articulated form, this strategy would have important Chinese economic and social benefits. It would contribute to the U.S.-China and economic relationship but it would also have deleterious impacts on U.S. national security.

As a matter of legal authority, export controls apply to the transfer of specific or general types of technology to foreign persons generally. In other words, their reach is not limited by law to a prescribed set of commercial circumstances—for example, corporate transactions.

The controls vary by technology type, end use and end user, and are designed to advance one or more national security foreign policy or other goals. The system is highly complex and nuanced.

As a matter of legal authority, CFIUS has legal jurisdiction over many but not all transactions. Three things must be true for a transaction to be a covered transaction and thus fall within CFIUS' jurisdiction.

First, the buyer or the investor has to be a foreign person, the transaction must be a controlled transaction, and the target business must be a U.S. business. All of these things are terms of art, and while CFIUS' reach is broad, it is not infinite.

Export controls and CFIUS have different, independently important, and complementary responsibilities. As Congress considers reforming one or both, it should focus its review primarily on gaps in resources and authorities.

I will end by saying U.S. technology leadership is essential, particularly with respect to certain emerging and foundational technologies to long-term U.S. national security interests.

To achieve this, the U.S. should pursue and not shrink from pursuing a whole of government strategy that does not rely exclusively on CFIUS and export controls or see these areas as the exclusive vectors of national security risk but builds strength on strength by countering illicit technology transfer however that may occur, enhancing the U.S.' economic competitiveness and technological superiority.

Thank you again for the opportunity to be with you today and for your commitment to exploring these important issues. I look forward to the committee's questions.

[The prepared statement of Mr. Mancuso follows:]

**U.S. Export Controls and the Committee on Foreign Investment in the United States
(CFIUS)**

**Testimony of the Honorable Mario Mancuso
Senior Visiting Fellow for International Security, The Hudson Institute
Partner, Kirkland & Ellis LLP**

Before the House Committee on Foreign Affairs

March 14, 2018

Chairman Royce, Ranking Member Engel, and other distinguished members of the Committee, thank you for the opportunity to testify this morning. I'm delighted to be with you, and with my distinguished fellow panelists.

My name is Mario Mancuso. Over the course of my career in government, I have had the privilege to serve in a variety of roles across the US national security and foreign policy enterprise, including as Under Secretary of Commerce for Industry and Security, Deputy Assistant Secretary of Defense for Special Operations and Combating Terrorism, a member of the Global Markets Board of the National Intelligence Council, and as a forward deployed military officer during *Operation Iraqi Freedom*.

In these roles, I learned a great deal about how US national security is conceived, debated and articulated in the interagency; how statecraft is operationalized; and how U.S. national security objectives are advanced "on the ground." I also learned a great deal about the difference between ideas and execution; inputs and outputs; the importance of legal authorities, resources and accountability; and the need for modesty, especially in presuming what we know and do not (and cannot) know and do.

Today, I am a Visiting Senior Fellow for International Security at the Hudson Institute, where I continue to work on questions relating to US strategy and statecraft in the emerging security environment. I am also a partner at Kirkland & Ellis LLP, where I advise clients with respect to matters that may implicate the US's national security regulation of international business activities, including with respect to CFIUS and export controls.

To be clear, I am here today in my personal capacity. The views I express here are mine alone, and should not be understood to be the views of Kirkland & Ellis or of its clients. I am here to offer some observations, in my capacity as a former government official, about these topics and to answer your questions about the imperative of US technology leadership, the international security profile and interests of the United States, and the role that CFIUS and export controls play in serving those interests. I will not discuss any specific case or matter that has been, or is currently before, the US government.

*****

As this Committee knows well, both CFIUS and export controls are important instruments of US national security statecraft. By design, they aim to effectuate a selective "denial strategy," which itself is premised on an important assumption: that the US has certain things that others want but do not have.

While globalization has rendered that assumption outdated in many areas, for certain emerging and foundational technologies (*e.g.*, artificial intelligence, robotics, augmented/ virtual reality, etc.) that assumption is still generally true.

On the other hand, while globalization has diminished our lead in certain technology areas, it has also been central to our economic and, by extension, our national security success. One need only look at US overmatch advantages in nuclear and electronics-enabled capabilities at critical junctures in our history to see how economic scale and technological superiority worked hand in hand in service of our global preeminence.

In this connection, as this Committee considers the contribution of CFIUS and export controls to US national security, I would invite the Committee to keep in mind two national security-related questions which may help frame its deliberations:

- At this time in our history, what is the optimal balance for the US to strike between economic openness and restrictiveness in order for the nation to secure the most important advantages of openness while mitigating its greatest risks?; and

- Whether, in light of that desired equilibrium, CFIUS and the current export control regime is, by virtue of their respective legal authorities and resources, properly configured to effectively implement and maintain this balance in the current environment?

In the interest of facilitating our discussion today, I wanted to offer some preliminary observations:

- Foreign direct investment (FDI) is critical to U.S. economic vitality. Not surprisingly for an advanced industrial economy, the largest proportion of FDI into the U.S. occurs as M&A activity. In the US, FDI accounts for approximately 7 million domestic jobs and other positive, ancillary economic impacts. The collective economic strength and vitality of our economy-- to which FDI clearly contributes-- helps resource our investments in national defense and extends our "soft-power" reach around the world.

- While the US remains a preferred global destination for FDI, our global share of FDI has declined in recent years. Because of its many direct and indirect benefits, this should be concerning to US policymakers, including US national security policymakers. Indeed, nations today must *compete* for FDI. A failure to consistently attract sufficient (benign) FDI into the US would present a long-term, systemic national security risk to the US.

- While FDI is generally good, certain transactions do, in fact, present transaction-specific national security risks. The policy question to consider in the context of FDI, therefore, is not primarily how to balance economics and national security interests, but how to balance systemic and transaction-specific national security risks.

- In recent years, strategic competition between the U.S. and China has increased across multiple domains--economic, political, and military. There is no reason to believe that such competition will abate in the coming years.

- China is actively pursuing a well-resourced, coordinated science and technology strategy that seeks to bolster "indigenous" Chinese innovation and to position China to be the world's technology and innovation leader. A number of pillars of this strategy are described in various official Chinese government pronouncements, such as "Made in China 2025", a number of Five-Year Plans, and certain published technology roadmaps. If successful in its articulated form, this strategy would have important Chinese economic and social benefits, contribute positively to the US-China economic relationship, *and* have deleterious impacts on US national security.

- Export controls have a long history in the US. In recent history, their defining policy challenge was during the Cold War, when they helped to manage strategic competition with the Soviet Union. During this period of Western solidarity and significant technological change, export controls worked reasonably well to prevent the illicit export of technology to Warsaw Pact countries. Since the Cold War, export controls have been significantly updated from time to time to address a broader set of US national security challenges. During this period, export controls have sought to balance, among other things, a complex bilateral relationship with China and the imperative to secure U.S. access to foreign technology markets in order to sustain scale economies to help fuel U.S. technology innovation, all against a backdrop of rapid and significant technological change and economic competition with strategic allies and others.

- As a matter of legal authority, export controls apply to the transfer of specific or general types of technology to foreign persons generally. In other words, their reach is not limited by law to a prescribed set of commercial circumstances (*e.g.*, a corporate transaction). The controls themselves vary by technology type, end-use and end-user, and are designed to advance one or more national security, foreign policy or other goals. The system is highly complex and nuanced.

- Historically, most FDI in the US came from Organization for Economic Cooperation and Development (OECD) countries, many of whom are formal US allies. By contrast, in recent years an increasing number of investors have come from Asia, especially China, as global liquidity has moved east. This macro-economic trend is generally considered a secular one and expected to continue, despite periodic political or cyclical economic volatility.

- As a matter of legal authority, CFIUS has legal jurisdiction over many, but not all, transactions. Three things must be true for a transaction to be a "covered transaction," and thus fall within CFIUS's jurisdictional perimeter: (a) the buyer or investor must be "foreign person"; (b) the transaction must be a "control" transaction; and (c) the target business must be a "US business." Each of these are terms of art, and broadly construed as a matter of agency practice. While CFIUS's reach is broad, it is not infinite.

- Export controls and CFIUS have different, independently important, and complementary responsibilities. As Congress considers reforming one or both, it should focus its review primarily on gaps in resources as well as legal authorities.

- US technology leadership is essential, particularly with respect to certain emerging and foundational technologies, to long-term US national security interests. To achieve this, the US should pursue a whole-of-government strategy that does not rely exclusively on CFIUS and export controls--or see these as the exclusive vectors of risk-- but builds "strength on strength" by countering illicit technology transfer (however that may occur) and enhancing the US's economic competitiveness and technological superiority.

Thank you, again, for the opportunity to be with you today, and for your commitment to exploring these important issues. I look forward to your questions.

Chairman ROYCE. Thank you, Mario.

We go to Ambassador Larson.

STATEMENT OF THE HONORABLE ALAN LARSON, SENIOR INTERNATIONAL POLICY ADVISOR, COVINGTON AND BURLING, LLP (FORMER UNDERSECRETARY FOR ECONOMIC, BUSINESS, AND AGRICULTURAL AFFAIRS, U.S. DEPARTMENT OF STATE)

Ambassador LARSON. Mr. Chairman, Mr. Engel, and distinguished members, I am delivering my testimony today on my personal responsibility, not on behalf of the organization where I work nor its clients.

Nevertheless, my views have been informed by over a dozen years at Covington and Burling and 32 years at the State Department. At each organization, I had responsibilities for CFIUS, trade controls, and sanctions.

As Congress considers CFIUS reform and export control reform including the export control——

Chairman ROYCE. Excuse me. Alan, here's a suggestion. Just pull the microphone a little closer. The people in the back indicate they couldn't hear it. There you go.

Ambassador LARSON. Is that okay? Thank you.

Chairman ROYCE. Ambassador, thank you.

Ambassador LARSON. As Congress considers reform of CFIUS and export control reforms like the Export Control Act, we should remember that the United States benefits greatly from foreign investment and foreign trade.

Foreign investment promotes economic dynamism, creates jobs, spurs innovation, and contributes to our ability to fund strong military and national security capabilities.

In my view, CFIUS works best when it focusses narrowly on protecting national security. Certain investments that give a foreign person control over a U.S. business can have national security implications.

CFIUS has been effective and adaptable in addressing such national security concerns. Other broader and vague economic goals such as economic security in my view should not replace national security as the standard for CFIUS.

Similarly, reciprocity or concerns about another county's trade policy, while very important issues, should be addressed by other policy tools and not by CFIUS.

Congress and the executive branch should regularly review, modernize, and reform CFIUS and export controls to address emerging national security risks. In the case of CFIUS, they did so in the Foreign Investment and National Security Act of 2007.

During the 10 years since FINSA was enacted, however, new security challenges have emerged. Today, China has become both an economic competitor and an economic partner of the United States.

In addition, China is both a strategic competitor of the United States and, at the same time, China works with the United States to promote certain shared security objectives including on con- taining the threat of North Korea's nuclear weapons and fighting terrorism.

U.S. policy should reflect the complexity and importance of our relationship with China. We should avoid actions that unnecessarily feed perception that we believe conflict between our countries is inevitable.

Now, China and the United States each have strong commercial reasons to pursue leadership and critical emerging technologies including artificial intelligence, semiconductors, and robotics, among others.

Some of these technologies have both commercial applications and also national security applications. As we consider the implications of these and other technologies on national security, we should very seriously consider reform and modernization of CFIUS in tandem with reform and modernization of U.S. export control regimes including the EAR and ITAR.

CFIUS and export control regimes can and should complement each other and be consistent with one another, not overlap and not contradict each other. Each regime, in my view, should focus on its areas of core expertise.

Other countries often criticize CFIUS and U.S. export controls and exaggerate their impact on legitimate commerce. My view is that the United States should do what we need to do to protect U.S. national security, notwithstanding such criticism and misunderstanding.

At the same time, we should take a clear-eyed, thoughtful, and balanced approach. We should protect national security in ways that promote economic dynamism at home. We should protect national security while avoiding to the maximum extent possible actions that unnecessarily foment misunderstandings.

The United States can and must build deeper and stronger economic and strategic cooperation with China while protecting national security and, in my opinion, we should see reform of CFIUS and of U.S. export control laws as complementary to such a clear-eyed strategy.

Thank you, Mr. Chairman.

[The prepared statement of Ambassador Larson follows:]

Principles for Reforming the Committee on Foreign Investment in the United States (CFIUS)

Statement by Alan Larson
Senior International Policy Advisor
Covington & Burling LLP

before the House Committee on Foreign Affairs
March 14, 2018

My name is Alan Larson. I am delivering testimony today on my personal responsibility. The views presented in this statement and my responses to the Committee's questions should not be taken as representing the views of my present employer, or of its clients.

My views have been informed by experiences during more than a dozen years in the private sector and thirty-two years in government. For the last twelve and a half years I have been a Senior International Policy Advisor at Covington, where my practice has focused on international investment, including transactions under the jurisdiction of the Committee on Foreign Investment in the United States (CFIUS), and on international trade and sanctions issues. Before joining Covington, I was a career Foreign Service Officer for thirty-two years. I was privileged to serve as Ambassador to the Organization for Economic Cooperation and Development (OECD) and, during the Bill Clinton and George W. Bush Administrations, in the top two economic policy jobs at the State Department--Assistant Secretary of State for Economic and Business Affairs and Under Secretary of State for Economic, Business and Agricultural Affairs. In those positions I oversaw the State Department's engagement on CFIUS, sanctions and export controls.

My testimony today will focus on CFIUS. In the Omnibus Trade Act of 1988, Congress gave the President the authority to review and investigate the acquisitions by a foreign person of a U.S. business when such acquisitions would give the foreign person control of that business. The President also was authorized to take actions necessary to protect against any negative impact on the national security of the United States arising from such transactions. This authority then was delegated to CFIUS, a delegation that Congress affirmed through the Foreign Investment and National Security Act of 2007 (FINSA).

Congress and successive administrations have recognized that the United States has benefitted greatly, and continues to benefit, from flows of foreign investment. These investments create jobs and economic activity in the United States. In doing so, foreign investment can contribute to the economic growth and dynamism that is essential to our ability to maintain technological leadership and to generate budgetary resources to fund the military and national security capabilities necessary to provide for our security.

Congress and successive administrations have determined that CFIUS works best when it is focused narrowly on protecting national security. At various times Congress and the executive branch have considered looser and broader standards, such as "economic security," but each time Congress and successive administrations have rejected such looser criteria.

Expanding the mandate of CFIUS to be an instrument of economic policy and to pursue economic goals would not, in my view, be consistent with the proper role or efficient functioning of CFIUS. For example, the principle of reciprocity has a role to play in the negotiation of trade and investment agreements. It is natural that the United States would insist on ensuring that such agreements provide a reasonable balance of benefits for all parties to the agreement. Investment reciprocity, however, is not an appropriate policy objective to pursue through CFIUS. If Congress or an Administration were to use CFIUS to pursue economic goals such as reciprocity, doing so would put CFIUS officials in the position of pursuing multiple objectives and surely undermine its effectiveness as a tool to protect national security.

For similar reasons, I believe using CFIUS as a tool or leverage in trade negotiations also would be a mistake. We have legitimate trade policy grievances and concerns with the trade policy conduct of other countries. Tough negotiations, the well-considered use of trade remedies like anti-dumping and countervailing duty laws and the deployment of other forms of WTO-consistent leverage all have a potential role to play in resolving such grievances and concerns. CFIUS, however, is a national security tool; its use as leverage in trade negotiations would confuse its objectives and make it less effective in accomplishing its core objective of protecting national security.

To be sure, CFIUS needs to be reviewed regularly and, as necessary, reformed and modernized to address emerging threats to national security. For example, a little more than a decade ago, Congress and the executive branch strengthened and enhanced the practices of CFIUS and, importantly, the accountability of CFIUS to Congress, through the Foreign Investment and National Security Act of 2007 (FINSA).

More than ten years after the enactment of FINSA, it is understandable that Congress and the Administration seek to review and consider steps to modernize and reform CFIUS. In my testimony, I will focus on geopolitical and technological changes that can motivate a review of CFIUS.

As one surveys the geopolitical arena, it is clear that the national security challenges facing the United States have evolved significantly during the last decade. China has emerged as an economic competitor, as well as an essential economic partner, of the United States. Naturally China and the United States each have a strong economic interest in developing and maintaining leadership positions in critical emerging technologies including artificial intelligence, semiconductors and robotics.

At the same time, China has become a potential strategic competitor of the United States. Scholars examining the sweep of history are now debating whether the "rise of China" can occur peacefully and in a manner that is consistent with the security interests of the United States. While China is a strategic competitor, it is equally true that China and the United States collaborate to address shared security concerns. For example, China and the United States have been working together to control risks such as those posed by an unrestrained, nuclear weapons-capable North Korea.

A review of changes during the last decade must include a recognition that many of the frontier technologies that appear to be vital for our future economic dynamism also appear to have significant implications for military capabilities and national security. Artificial intelligence, semiconductors and robotics have both commercial and national security applications.

There is broad agreement that technological innovation makes a crucial and indispensable contribution to the economic vitality of the United States, as well as to our military superiority. We need to preserve and promote innovation at home. We need to encourage more U.S. students to pursue science, technology, engineering and mathematics (STEM) studies and we need to welcome immigrants with those skills. We need to maintain an environment conducive to the continued leadership of world class universities operating on the frontiers of these fields.

We also need to ensure that technologies crucial for national security, including dual use technologies, are not pirated, stolen or leaked to potential adversaries. I am personally sensitive to this responsibility; when I served as the Ambassador of the United States to the OECD, I was also responsible for delegations to the Coordinating Committee for Multilateral Export Controls (COCOM), an international organization that helped the United States restrict the flow of militarily sensitive technologies to adversaries.

The question arises as to the role CFIUS should play and how this role would, in the case of dual use technologies, complement but not compete nor conflict with the Export Administration Regulations (EAR). In the case of military technologies, CFIUS should complement but not compete nor conflict with the International Traffic in Arms Regulations (ITAR). It would be natural that a tune-up and modernization of CFIUS would be complemented by a tune-up of trade controls. The operations of CFIUS and of U.S. trade controls regimes should be complementary and consistent, not overlapping and contradictory.

As an initial matter, CFIUS already has the jurisdiction to review foreign acquisitions that would give the investor control of a company possessing a technology critical to the defense posture of the United States. Any new authorities in this space should be carefully crafted to take into account the expertise of executive branch export control officials and the regulatory roles of the EAR and ITAR. Any new authorities should be crafted in a way that promotes clarity and certainty. They should provide clear timelines, not overload the system and ensure continued accountability to the Congress. Any new rules should recognize that foreign investment in frontier technologies can be crucial to the development of these technologies. When such investments are verifiably undertaken as purely passive investments seeking a purely financial return, they should be welcomed.

As Congress reviews CFIUS and trade controls authorities, it will be necessary to ensure that U.S. laws and regulations adequately protect national security while not unnecessarily inhibiting productive foreign investments, exports or new business arrangements. My starting point would be to build on the core strengths established in CFIUS, the EAR and ITAR. If the goal is to regulate new forms of potential exports of dual use or military technology to other countries, I would look first to the EAR and ITAR, with experts at the Department of Defense, Department of State and Department of Commerce, as the institutions most likely to address these risks effectively. Similarly, to address potential new national security risks arising from inward foreign investment, I would look first to CFIUS, which has had remarkable success in evolving its procedures to meeting new challenges.

As previous witnesses in other hearings have testified, the workload of CFIUS has grown rapidly in recent years, putting stress on the system. Any expansion of the mandate of the Committee should be considered with great care to avoid distracting the focus of CFIUS and reducing its effectiveness in carrying out its core mission.

It is important to manage the resources of CFIUS efficiently, so that it focuses especially intensely on transactions that are the most complex and may pose the most serious potential risks to national security. For this reason, I see merit in proposals for a "short form" CFIUS declarations that could be filed to determine whether CFIUS has sufficient interest or concern to merit a full review.

It is important that CFIUS not block transactions that could proceed without inappropriate risk to national security, so long as the parties commit to and conscientiously implement an effective and enforceable mitigation agreement. Such mitigation agreements are essential in preventing CFIUS from unnecessarily inhibiting foreign investment. Because the government must devote resources to the negotiation, monitoring and enforcement of such mitigation agreements, I support appropriate measures to augment CFIUS budgetary and staffing resources and to assure that "user charges" may be applied wherever possible to ensure that the parties to the transaction bear a fair share of the costs.

As a diplomat and a policy advisor at a law firm, I have observed that CFIUS and U.S. export control laws and regulations are widely misunderstood and heavily criticized abroad. Other countries often greatly exaggerate their impact on legitimate trade and investment. A certain amount of this misunderstanding, criticism and exaggeration is inevitable and I accept it as the price we pay for taking necessary steps to protect U.S. national security.

At the same time, we should seek to minimize unwarranted misunderstanding and criticism and we should make genuine efforts to demonstrate that we welcome legitimate foreign investment. While we recognize, and will take action to protect against, new risks to national security, we also should recognize that legitimate foreign investment generates economic activity, creates jobs, spurs innovation and generates economic growth and budget revenues essential for national security. We should do everything reasonable to show that the United States genuinely welcomes such foreign investment. We must avoid imposing barriers that gratuitously convey the message foreign investors are not welcome.

Taking a clear-eyed, thoughtful and balanced approach toward the review, reform and modernization of CFIUS and export controls is necessary to protect U.S. national security. Acting in a clear-eyed, thoughtful and balanced way is equally necessary if we seek to sustain a dynamic and growing domestic economy. And as a former diplomat, I cannot stress too strongly that a clear-eyed, thoughtful and balanced approach also is necessary to avoid fomenting misunderstandings that could feed the false idea that conflict between China and the United States is inevitable.

A study of the past suggests that significant shifts in the geopolitical balance of power led to conflict when great powers misunderstood the other's goals and intentions. We can learn from the past. We can, must and will do what we need to do to protect national security. At the same time, we can and should work diligently to build deeper and stronger economic and strategic cooperation with China. Reform and modernization of CFIUS and export control laws should be seen, in my opinion, within the frame of reference of such a policy towards China.

Chairman ROYCE. Thank you, Alan.
Mr. Wolf.

STATEMENT OF THE HONORABLE KEVIN WOLF, PARTNER, AKIN GUMP STRAUSS HAUER AND FELD, LLP (FORMER ASSISTANT SECRETARY FOR EXPORT ADMINISTRATION, BUREAU OF INDUSTRY AND SECURITY, U.S. DEPARTMENT OF COMMERCE)

Mr. WOLF. Thank you, Chairman, Ranking Member for holding this hearing, for introducing the bill, raising the topic. Thanks also to Senators Cornyn, Feinstein, and Congressman Pittenger for raising the issue in their bill as well.

This is a very important topic, and from my time in the government I agree that the underlying motives and concerns to be addressed by each of the bills and the topics should be addressed and they're real and legitimate, and this has been a terrific example of a quality public debate on a very serious difficult issue.

By the way also, the views I express today are my own and not on behalf of my firm or any of its clients.

So I think most people agree with the underlying issue to be addressed and the concern that you described well in your opening statement. The issue is how best to address it in a way that does more good than harm.

And in general, with export controls and CFIUS there are two primary approaches that are being discussed and one approach is a very broad open-ended scope of controls or investment authorities that is safe that catches large numbers of transactions and one decides later whether there is a transaction of concern or technology to be transferred that would be of concern.

And the other approach is a much more tailored specific set of controls where the government does the hard work up front to identify what the threats are and to address the controls more directly with fewer collateral consequences, less uncertainty, and less harm to foreign direct investment.

So my role, in my view, is that to the extent that any of the concerns that are being discussed in either of the bills deal with technologies of concern that are not now controlled by the export control system but that should be. The best way to address it is through the existing export control authorities.

Very simply, all of export controls can really be reduced down to one sentence. They are the set of rules that govern the export, re-export, and transfer of technology, software, services, and hardware to specific end uses, to specific destinations, and to specific end users for various national security and foreign policy purposes.

That's my entire professional life in one sentence. I feel very small all of a sudden.

Anyway, within the Export Administration regulations there are lots of tools to address each of these issues depending upon what the threat is in very tailored ways to avoid unintended consequences and strains on government resources.

The rules are capable of being adapted unilaterally and quickly for emerging technologies that are of concern that weren't identified as part of our list review efforts.

They are capable of addressing specific end uses, specific end users, and specific destinations. The descriptions of the technology and the types of information that could be captured and controlled by these regulations is infinitely variable, going from at its earliest stages of information and developmental technology or know-how and leading up all the way through production and operation and use technology.

So to go right to the answer to the question of this hearing—how do we best address and regulate cutting-edge technologies for national security reasons—frankly, I think the answer is in your bill in Section 109 and it lays out a process of requiring the government, through an interagency process, drawing upon all of the experts that are within the government and outside the government and industry and academia to identify what the threats are and what the choke point technologies and other information are to address the concerns that you well described in your opening; to publish those as drafts so that industry has a chance to review it and comment on it, to avoid unintended consequences and to make sure that it's clear and understandable; if it's an emergency situation use the existing authorities within the Export Administration regulations, to tag those and control those technologies immediately but to the extent it is not an emergency, work with our interagency friends to submit to the multilateral regimes, these same technologies, so that our allies are controlling it as well for the same reason; to support and fund the administration of these regulations for education and outreach and for very aggressive enforcement of the controls for a level playing field; and then have a process in place to regular review and update the controls as threats and technologies evolve.

This bill—the statutory authority for this system—was last addressed 40 years ago. The world is a very different place now than it was then. And so I applaud the members in this committee for raising this topic and moving forward.

And with that, I am happy to answer whatever thoughts or questions you might have.

[The prepared statement of Mr. Wolf follows:]

United States House Committee on Foreign Affairs
"Modernizing Export Controls: Protecting Cutting-Edge Technology and U.S.
National Security"

Prepared Remarks of The Honorable Kevin J. Wolf
Partner, Akin Gump Strauss Hauer & Feld LLP
Former Assistant Secretary of Commerce for Export Administration (2010-2017)

March 14, 2018

Chairman Royce, Ranking Member Engel, and other distinguished members of the committee. Thank you for convening this hearing and for inviting me to testify on this important national security topic. It is a pleasure being back before the committee.

For nearly 25 years in both the private sector and government, I have focused my practice on the law, policy, and administration of export control and related foreign direct investment issues. From 2010 to 2017, I was the Assistant Secretary of Commerce for Export Administration. In this role, I was primarily responsible for the policy and administration of the U.S. dual-use export control system and, as a result of the Export Control Reform effort I helped lead, part of the defense trade system. I was also during this time a Commerce Department representative to the Committee on Foreign Investment in the United States (CFIUS), particularly with respect to cases involving technology transfer issues.

Although I am now a partner at Akin Gump Strauss Hauer & Feld LLP, the views I express today are my own. I am not advocating for or against any issue or potential changes to legislation on behalf of another. Rather, I am here to answer your questions about how the export control system works, how it should be modernized to protect cutting-edge technologies that warrant controls for national security reasons, and any other related policy topic you would like to discuss.

What are Export Controls?

Export controls are the rules that govern

> (i) the export, reexport, and transfer
> (ii) by U.S. and foreign persons
> (iii) of commodities, information/technology, software, and services
> (iv) to destinations, end users, and end uses
> (v) to accomplish various national security and foreign policy objectives.

That is my entire professional life in one sentence. Although it appears deceptively simple, each export control decision requires complex, multivariate policy and legal analyses involving statutes, regulations, international commitments, intelligence and law enforcement equities, threat assessments, industrial base implications, license administration, budgets/resources, corporate compliance considerations, foreign availability, interagency dynamics, congressional concerns, and multilateral and bilateral foreign policy issues. The technologies are often complex, evolving, and wide ranging, including everything from information about bird flu to machine tools to items that are being invented today that most do not understand. Technologies that were once sensitive become ubiquitous, such as the GPS technology in our cell phones. Generally non-sensitive commercial technologies can be applied to new uses or by end users of concern in ways that are harmful to our interests. Most extraordinarily advanced technologies, however, represent no threat whatsoever. But many simple, old technologies, such as those unique to standard military equipment, warrant controls for most of the world. Concerns about destinations, end users, and end uses vary widely and change constantly.

Controls Should be Tailored to Address the National Security Concern

National security concerns are, of course, paramount and should be the basis for any final decisions. The United States never wants to be in a fair fight. The appropriate, aggressively enforced, clearly written, and *well-funded* export and related controls are a critical part of maintaining that advantage. I have never subscribed to the view that export controls should "balance" national security concerns with economic concerns. National security concerns are not to be traded off for something else in a particular transaction or in trade deals. Rather, they should be properly calibrated, tailored controls to avoid collateral economic costs, unnecessary regulatory burdens, and misallocation of federal resources. Excessive controls harm the U.S. defense industrial base, which results in harm to our national security. Lax, out of date, or poorly enforced controls have the same effect.

Export controls are *not* the solution to all policy concerns. They are also not tools for industrial policy. They should be used to their fullest possible extent, however, when a national security issue pertains to the export, reexport, or transfer of commodities, technologies, software or services to destinations, end users, or end uses. If the issue pertains to an activity, an investment, or a concern separate from such events, then one must look to other areas of law, such as sanctions, trade remedies, foreign direct investment controls, intellectual property theft remedies, or counter-espionage laws.

The "Four Singles" Idea

Many parts of the U.S. Government regulate the export of items for various reasons. As discussed many times during my government tenure, my view is that the administration of the export control system should be consolidated under one roof, under one set of regulations, with one information technology and online licensing system, and one export enforcement coordinating authority. Such a system would accomplish our national security and foreign policy objectives more efficiently and with dramatically fewer regulatory burdens. It should, of course, draw upon the expertise and equities of all relevant federal agencies and industry experts when deciding what to control where and how, but why impose on industry and the government different rules, different words, different forms, and different procedures to accomplish the same goal? That was not to be, however, and will have to wait for another day to be considered again.

The Bureau of Industry and Security (BIS) and the Export Administration Regulations (EAR)

For purposes of today's hearing, though, the system at issue is the one managed by the Department of Commerce's Bureau of Industry and Security (BIS), which administers the Export Administration Regulations (EAR). These regulations govern the items that warrant control but that are not regulated by another part of the U.S. Government. In essence, they describe on the Commerce Control List (CCL) the commercial, dual-use, and less sensitive military items that warrant control for national security, foreign policy, and other reasons.

BIS and the EAR also play an important role in furthering and complementing the foreign-policy based sanctions and embargoes administered by the Treasury Department. The EAR also contains Short Supply control authority and anti-boycott regulations. These issues, however, are not the topic of today's hearing. Also not subject to today's hearing are the International Traffic in Arms Regulations (ITAR), administered by the State Department. They regulate sensitive military items under the authority of the Arms Export Control Act.

The authority for the relevant parts of the EAR rests upon a 2001 Executive Order and annual presidential notices continuing the emergency need for the regulations under the authority of the International Emergency Economic Powers Act (IEEPA). As properly stated by the Chairman and Ranking Member, The Export Control Reform Act of 2018 (H.R. 5040) is the first real push to establish *permanent* authority for the EAR since the Cold War-era Export Administration Act (EAA) of 1979 expired in 2001. My personal view is that the bill's statement of policy in section 102 for this part of the export control system is perfect.[1] I applaud the members for addressing this issue. Many of the threats and technologies are very different now than they were in 1979 and the issue warrants evaluation more frequently than every 40 years.

What are Dual-Use Technologies and Why Regulate Them?

This reality gets right to the heart of the title of this hearing – how are cutting-edge dual-use technologies that warrant control identified and regulated? "Dual-use" items – *i.e.*, commodities, software, and technology – are those that have both benign commercial applications as well as applications of concern, such as those pertaining to military applications and weapons of mass destruction. The machine tool that can be used to make a commercial aircraft part could also be used to make a missile skin. The

---

[1] I did, however, notice what appear to be unintentional drafting errors in the bill with respect to, for example, the definition of "U.S. Person" and the scope of foreign items that could be subject to the jurisdiction of the regulations. I will suggest technical fixes to staff after the hearing.

microelectronic circuit that is important for a cellular phone network might be critical to a military radar.

As this core definition indicates, not everything that is cutting edge or emerging warrants control. In fact, most such technologies clearly do not. So, a government must work backwards and identify the threats first. What are the technologies and other items, real and prospective, that will maintain the United States' military and intelligence advantages over other countries and adversaries? What are the technologies and items that others seek or are likely to seek to eliminate that advantage? What are the foreign policy considerations, including human rights concerns, that warrant imposing controls? In short, the answer to the question is that the export control system gets such input and information from multiple sources and Commerce's BIS coordinates its implementation in to a regulatory, licensing, education, and enforcement system.

Which Parts of the Government Constitute the Dual-Use Export Control System?

The Defense Department, including its services, labs, and many experts, has a significant, if not primary, responsibility for identifying such technologies. The **Defense Technology Security Administration (DTSA)** is DoD's point of contact for the export control system and makes DoD's recommendations pertaining to foreign access to U.S. technology and other items. The National Security Agency's Industry and Academic Engagement group provides technical support to BIS regarding controls over the export of encryption.

The State Department's **Bureau of International Security and Nonproliferation (ISN)** leads the department's efforts to prevent the spread of WMD and their delivery systems. It is the export control system's point of contact for the State Department's expertise in these areas and the department's foreign policy assessments of transactions. ISN is also the leader of the interagency efforts to coordinate and revise U.S. export controls with those of our multilateral export control regime partners in The Wassenaar Arrangement (conventional arms and dual-use items), the Nuclear Suppliers Group, the Australia Group (chemical and biological weapons), and the Missile Technology Control Regime. Through such efforts, the United States is able to propose and get coordinated controls among allies and others on technologies and other items of common concern. It also benefits through this system from the expertise and insights of our regime allies in identifying items of concern, including emerging technologies.

The **National Nuclear Security Administration (NNSA)** coordinates the input and expertise of the Department of Energy, primarily pertaining to matters involving nuclear science, into the dual-use export control system.

The Commerce Department's **Bureau of Industry and Security (BIS)** is responsible for reducing all such efforts, input, and expertise into the content and administration of the EAR. It is the point of the contact for the Commerce Department's views on export controls and responsible for running an efficient, coherent, reliable, enforceable, and predictable export control system, including resolving competing agency views or policy objectives. Its mission statement (which includes more than just export control issues) is at: https://www.bis.doc.gov/index.php/about-bis/mission-statement. Its licensing officers and other officials are experts in their areas of responsibility and generally have engineering, scientific, military, intelligence, or foreign policy backgrounds. Export control rules are inherently complex. To ensure that they achieve their objectives, and to reduce unnecessary regulatory burdens (particularly on small- and medium-sized businesses), BIS's mission includes the provision of a substantial amount of industry education and outreach. BIS also has its own enforcement authorities and an Office of Export Enforcement (OEE) with special agents focused on investigating and, in close coordination with the Department of Justice, the Federal Bureau of Investigation, and the Department of Homeland Security, enforcing the EAR. OEE is also BIS's point of contact with the intelligence community and provides input on licensing determinations.

Thus, DTSA, ISN, NNSA, and BIS are the responsible reviewing agencies for dual-use export control determinations, including decisions to list, revise, or remove a control, as well as case-by-case decisions on individual applications seeking a license to engage in a controlled activity. Although not part of the dual-use licensing system, BIS coordinates with the State Department's Directorate of Defense Trade Controls (DDTC) to prevent jurisdictional overlap with the sensitive military items subject to its control. In addition, BIS draws upon the expertise of other parts of the U.S. Government as needed, such as the Department of Homeland Security, National Institutes of Health, and the National Aeronautics and Space Administration.

Finally, BIS has technical advisory committees of industry experts in the technology areas for which BIS is responsible. They provide industry input into new technologies and new applications of old technologies to help BIS further its mission. The members have security clearances and have the authority to meet in both public and non-public sessions. They are a vital tool for BIS to use when identifying emerging technologies of concern.

The Export Control Reform (ECR) Effort

During the Obama Administration, all this expertise was applied in a massive seven-year effort involving hundreds of experts and affecting tens of thousands of items to review and substantially update the lists of military items. The goal was to identify and distinguish between those items that provide the United States with a critical or significant military advantage, and those that are less sensitive. If an item was identified as being militarily critical, important, or unique, it was listed on either the State Department's U.S. Munitions List or the Commerce Department's list of new military controls, and controlled according to its sensitivity.

Our national security was enhanced as a result of this effort because it (i) helped to increase military interoperability with our NATO and other close allies, (ii) helped the defense and space industrial base by reducing the incentives for allies to design out or avoid U.S.-origin content, (iii) made the rules more reliable and predictable, and (iv) allowed the government to focus its resources more on transactions, end uses, end users, and destinations of concern. The background to this fourth point is that too many government resources were devoted to reviewing and approving transactions of less sensitive items in the allied supply chain (that were never denied), when we should have been focusing more of our attention on the more sensitive items and trade involving the countries, end uses, end users of more concern.

Emerging and other items of concern identified as a result of this effort were evaluated and led to amendments of dual-use controls and changes to the international control lists. Our experience with microwave monolithic integrated circuits (MMICs) is a perfect example of this process. MMICs have long been important parts of military radar systems. As a result of the reform effort, the government learned more about their commercial technology evolution and large number of non-military applications, such as with respect to commercial telecommunications systems. This work led to substantial revisions of the military and dual-use controls, both in the United States and in the regimes, over such items.

So that the revised military controls stayed current, we set in motion a process requiring each of the categories to be evaluated every two years or so to account for evolutions in technology, commercialization, and new threats. The system would also be user friendly in that it would correct mistakes and, based on the past experience, find ways of describing the controls more clearly. The Trump Administration has continued this effort and is now, for example, beginning the process of getting industry and government input on how controls on military electronics and other items should be updated.

This is not to say that we did not review and revise the dual-use controls during the reform effort. To the contrary, there were substantial revisions to these controls over the years, primarily as a part of the regular efforts to revise and update the multilateral export control lists. It is, however, a fair comment that we devoted extra efforts to identifying and describing better controls on military items and only traditional efforts to identifying and describing new commercial technologies that could be of concern. We often said that we wanted to do a top-to-bottom scrub of the dual-use controls at the same level of intensity we were doing for military controls, but military priorities and resource constraints did not permit it.

Renewed Attention to Unlisted Commercial Emerging Technologies of Possible Concern

It is for this reason that I compliment Congressmen Royce and Engel for highlighting the need for such an effort in their export control bill. I also compliment Senator Cornyn, Senator Feinstein, Congressman Pittenger, and all the other co-sponsors of the Foreign Investment Risk Review Modernization Act (FIRRMA), and the Administration, for highlighting and creating a robust public debate over the best ways to identify and regulate the transfer of emerging critical technologies of concern that are not yet controlled but that should be.

These legislative discussions have clearly given a kick to the system to be sure that it does not get too comfortable with evaluating just the traditional WMD, military, and dual-use technologies of concern that it knows about. The system should put in extra outside-the-box efforts with experts not normally part of the export control system to study emerging technologies in commercial sectors that it may not ordinarily come across. I do not now have recommendations for which specific emerging technologies are not now controlled but should be, but I am confident that a regular interagency process focused on this topic that draws upon all available experts will get to the best answer.

How long it will take to get to such answers is a function of the resources put into the effort and the creativity of those involved. Even with massive attention and resources, however, the task will not be an easy one. The several specific emerging technologies, such as additive manufacturing and driverless vehicle technology, that we studied for possible controls during my time proved to be particularly difficult in revealing which parts or subsets warranted controls to address an actual or possible treat. Clamping down too hard on an emerging technology will drive research and development in the areas offshore, which hurts our national security. Not controlling it enough can result in the shrinking of the military and intelligence advantages we have that I discussed earlier.

Current Authorities to Control Unlisted Emerging Technologies of Concern

That we did not have a regular, separate research effort focused on emerging commercial technologies does not mean we were not thinking about the issue. Indeed, we were so concerned about the possibility of inadvertently missing something during the military list review effort or later discovering a new technology of concern that we wanted to make sure we had the authority to regulate it quickly and without hassle. This is why I and my colleagues at BIS created a novel tool in the EAR to allow us to quickly and unilaterally control emerging and other unlisted technologies that warranted control, so long as the technology was eventually submitted to the relevant regimes to be controlled multilaterally.[2] This is referred to as the "0Y521" series of controls in the EAR, which mirrors similar authority in U.S. Munitions List Category XXI in the State Department's International Traffic in Arms Regulations.[3]

Thus, if BIS or any other agency identified a previously uncontrolled technology that warranted control because its uncontrolled release could harm our national security or foreign policy interests, BIS could impose controls on its export, reexport, and transfer immediately without needing to wait for a public notice and comment process or getting consensus among the multilateral regime partners. This is a short-term fix because the best controls are those that benefit from industry input (to ensure that the descriptions are clear and without unintended consequences) and that are controlled similarly by the allies (to further the common objectives of the controls and to level the playing field). Nonetheless, the authority exists today to control immediately emerging technologies of

---

[2] See 77 Fed. Reg. 22191 (Apr. 13, 2012).
[3] See 22 C.F.R. § 121.1.

concern at any stage of their development once someone in the government identifies the technology in a way that can be reduced to regulatory control text and can provide the required national security or foreign policy justification for the control.

A key element to this control (and ideally, all controls) is that the scope is clear. Vague descriptions of what is controlled that leave exporters and foreign parties uncertain about what is within the control harm both compliance objectives and impose unnecessary economic harms. For regulations to work, all parties involved must know what and is not captured by a control. Uncertainty discourages otherwise legitimate exports and imposes compliance costs on companies that need to analyze the transaction longer than necessary.

The EAR Has Many Tools Available for Addressing National Security and Foreign Policy Concerns

Not all concerns pertaining to technology are best addressed through identifying it on a control list for general controls. Sometimes, the technology as such is not the issue, but its application by specific end users is the concern. That is, BIS, through intelligence or other sources, comes across information that a particular end user is going to put otherwise non-sensitive or old technology to a bad end use. The EAR allows for tailored controls to specific end users, such as through the "is informed" process and the Entity List process. This means that BIS can inform particular parties that specific exports are of concern and require authorizations without imposing burdens on all other exports of the same technology. The Entity List process allows BIS to add particular foreign entities to lists that, in the main, result in a prohibition on the export of all items, listed and unlisted, from the United States. This can create economic incentives for the listed entities, which are generally outside United States jurisdiction, to stop engaging in acts contrary to our national security and foreign policy interests. The EAR also imposes controls on otherwise uncontrolled items if they are destined for end uses of concern, such as WMD applications worldwide or military end uses in China or Russia. Finally, the EAR allows for prohibitions on activities of US persons if they are for WMD-related activities, even if items subject to the regulations are not involved.

Thus, the EAR is clearly and deliberately not a "one-size-fits-all" type of regulation, which is its virtue and its vice. It is a virtue because it allows for tailored controls to address the concern at issue without imposing unnecessary regulatory and economic burdens on transactions not of concern. That is, paradoxically, also its vice because, with tailored controls, comes complexity and the need for the government do to the hard work up front of identifying what the threats are and regulate for them thereafter. Controls that regulate everything equally everywhere all the time are safe and easy to create -- and absolutely needed for military crown jewels and inherently critical items -- but, for all other items, impose many collateral burdens that do more harm than good.

The EAR Controls Are Tailored to Different Types of Items

The inherent complexity in the EAR is magnified when considering that its controls include physical items, software, and technology – and the technology controls are further divided primarily among developmental technology, production technology, and use technology. Often the technology is more of a concern than a physical item and developmental technology is of more concern than operational technology. Moreover, the descriptions of technology in the regulations can be as broad or as narrow as the national security or foreign policy concerns warrant. They are generally connected to physical commodities, but do not need to be. They could be based on a technology's technical parameters, end uses, stage of development, or merely just a reference to the name of the technology.

After a technology or other item is identified, the controls on its transfer can be tailored in the regulations to apply to the whole world or to specific destinations, end uses, and end users to address specific concerns. The control choice is a function of a national security and foreign policy judgment to be made on a technology-by-technology basis and regardless of the existence or nature of any underlying commercial transaction. That is, export controls apply to exports or other releases regardless of, for example, whether the exporter is owned or controlled by a foreign parent, the transaction is sale or a joint venture, or the release is tangible or intangible.

Effective, Well-Funded Enforcement is Critical to the Success of the System

The effort to identify emerging and other technologies of concern, describe them in the regulations, and educate the public about them, however, is meaningless unless there is effective enforcement of the controls – and unless law enforcement officials have the tools they need to do their jobs. There are regular interdiction efforts of items destined to an end use or end user of concern. There are on-site audits in the U.S. and abroad that stop illegal acts before they occur. There are undercover efforts and stings. There are tips provided by commercial competitors and allies about likely violations. There is a long list of criminal prosecutions of export control violations to prove these and related points.

The system, however, *like most regulated areas*, largely relies on voluntary compliance motivated by a fear of being subject to painful civil or criminal penalties for non-compliance. It is impossible for the government to review every transfer of technology from or outside the United States and the contents of every box going through a U.S. or foreign port. Most technology transfers are intangible and the tangible volumes are massive and overwhelmingly not items of national security concern. Robust export control law enforcement is thus needed to motivate those on the front lines of exporting from the United States and *reexporting controlled items outside the United States* to develop and maintain comprehensive programs to ensure compliance with the rules, regardless of whether the company is domestic or owned by a foreign entity. I know it may seem counter-intuitive to think that industry should advocate for well-resourced, level-headed law enforcement, but it is actually critical to keeping the playing field level for those companies that do the hard work to stay compliant.

Given the inherent complexity in the system, it is also critical that there is a core group of enforcement officials specially trained and focused on export control enforcement – and that the public knows they have all the tools and resources they need to do their jobs. Although the full law enforcement resources of the U.S. government are absolutely needed to motivate compliance, the topic is not one to be left exclusively to enforcement officials distracted by other priorities. Law enforcement personnel dedicated to export control compliance are also often better able to work with their foreign counterparts to ensure joint efforts to identify and stop export control violations outside the United States. Such a group, by the way, already exists in BIS's Office of Export Enforcement.

The Existing System Works Well, but Could Benefit from More Resources and Attention to Novel Issues

In my experience, the existing export control system works well. BIS and its sister agencies are full of talented, dedicated, and motivated public officials. Given the (legitimate) increase in attention to analyzing emerging technologies, at whatever stage of their development, more resources are needed for them to do this work on top of their regular efforts. I make this polite suggestion not only for their benefit but also for the sake of our national security.

On every export control issue, I have a three-minute, a thirty-minute, a three-hour, and a three-day version. So, I will stop here with a summary answer to the core question of this hearing, which is how do we control cutting-edge technologies to protect our national security? The answer is in section 109 of your bill, which, in sum, says:

1. enhance the existing export control system with a regular, well-funded interagency effort to get from national security and intelligence experts not normally part of the system information and predictions regarding new technologies that are critical to maintaining our military and intelligence advantages;

2. identify the types of technologies, at whatever stage of their development, that are necessary to maintain such advantages;

3. absent an emergency need to publish unilateral controls immediately, publish proposed amendments to the export control rules for public comment to make sure they are clear and do not contain unintended collateral consequences unrelated to or that would harm our national security;

4. publish final controls tailored to the destinations, end uses, and end users of concern, regardless of the nature of the underlying transaction;

5.   educate the U.S. and foreign public, and our allies, on the controls and the reasons for why they are needed;

6.   work with the relevant regimes to develop common, multilateral controls over the new technologies – *i.e.*, so that the technologies are controlled by allies outside the United States as well as when sent from the United States;

7.   provide healthy resources and tools to the law enforcement agencies so that they can properly investigate and prosecute violations of the new and the old controls; and

8.   institutionalize a system to regularly review, revise, and update the controls so that they do not become outdated.

Thank you again for spending the time to think through this complex and important national security issue. I am happy to answer whatever questions you have.

The Structure of All US Export Control Law

Act: Export, Reexport, or Transfer **Actor:** US Person or Foreign Person (people and companies)	Physical Things ("Goods," "Commodities," "Defense Articles")	Information ("Technology," Technical Data")	Software	Services ("defense services" or WMD-related "activities")	Transactions (e.g., agreements or transferring money)
Destinations (Countries or regions, for listed items, or embargoed destinations for all else)					
End-Uses (e.g., WMD end uses regardless of item's classification)					
End-Users (e.g., SDNs or Listed Entities, regardless of item's classification)					

Chairman ROYCE. Mr. Wolf, thank you, and for the committee members here the reason Eliot and I have introduced this bill is— this new export control statute is because the Export Administra- tion Act, which has been around for a long time, it was designed to handle trade controls on the Soviet bloc.

So that was before most of the members were on this committee. And it's never been comprehensively updated since then.

It's been in lapse, actually, for most of the last quarter century and as a result what we've done is we've had to rely on emergency authorities to uphold our dual use and that's why we are focused on this legislation.

As Mr. Wolf noted, it is key to control emerging critical tech- nologies that may become essential to national security. The Export Control Reform Act that we've got here before us on the committee would explicitly assign this authority to U.S. export control agen- cies.

So I will ask Ambassador Larson first. Are you concerned at all that attempting to control emerging critical technologies primarily through an expanded CFIUS process may negatively impact U.S. innovation and, indirectly, technology advantage?

Ambassador LARSON. Well, thank you, Mr. Chairman.

I think that one of the things I learned in government was that we were usually most effective if we had used the parts of our Gov- ernment that had the expertise and knowledge to lead.

And so in respect of controlling and export or transfer of critical U.S. technologies, my first point of emphasis would be on the ex- port control regimes that we've used in the past.

I support the idea that those need to be updated to take into ac- count the changed geopolitical situation, the changed technological situation. But I think that's the first way to start.

I think CFIUS does a good job on its mandate and its mandate has been to ensure that there are not acquisitions by a foreign per- son of control of a U.S. company that would impair the national se- curity; and that can include instances where that U.S. company has critical technology and I think CFIUS has handled that respon- sibility well.

Chairman ROYCE. I think they're complementary but I think we've got to have export controls——

Ambassador LARSON. Precisely.

Chairman ROYCE [continuing]. In statute and that's what we are focused on.

Ambassador LARSON. Precisely.

Chairman ROYCE. So here's another question and I will ask this one of Mr. Mancuso or Mr. Wolf.

If one of the most pressing concerns driving this debate is tech- nology transfer to China, could U.S. export controls be tailored to address this national security concern without excessively impact trade with other countries or without creating undue uncertainty about whether other transactions could come within the scope of CFIUS review?

Mr. Wolf, if you'd like, sir.

Mr. WOLF. Yes, absolutely. That's my primary point about the beauty of the export control system in that it is infinitely tailorable to address specific technologies at whatever stage of their concern—at whatever stage of their development that are of concern for transfer to specific end users or specific destinations or for spe- cific applications and that way once you identify what the threat— once the national security experts identify what the concerns are that would harm our national security in terms of altering our edge on a variety of different areas you can, through the export control system, either unilaterally or multilaterally or both identify those technologies specifically and clearly and tailor them in such a way so that it doesn't affect the types of transactions or countries or end users which are not a threat, particularly with respect to the allies. To the extent that the concern is not related to technology trans- fer, then the export control system may not be your best vehicle and other tools such as the espionage rules or the IT theft rules or CFIUS for other topics should come into play.

But I agree with the essence of your question completely.

Chairman ROYCE. And Mario, do you concur?

Mr. MANCUSO. So, Chairman Royce, I do concur but I would like to add some additional detail because I certainly think that the ex- port control regime has the existing authority, has built within it the capacity to be flexible and fast and all the things that Kevin mentioned.

But I would point out that, as a practical matter, in the execu- tion of these responsibilities the system operates very differently today.

So, for example, even the taxonomy of creating CIFs between destination, end user and end use, kind of suggests the Cold War and 9/11 era thinking around export controls and products outside the United States.

I think the fact of the matter is that for some of these emerging technologies that transfer is occurring within the United States.

So while I agree the authorities are broad enough, I am not sure the resources are there or the practice sufficiently developed that we focus on illicit tech transfer inside the United States because I think that's critical and that's fundamentally different than the Cold War.

One other point, Chairman Royce, if I may. The other thing that's difficult is during the Cold War we—our U.S.—there was tre- mendous agreement with U.S. strategic allies about the Cold War threat and at the time our strategic allies were not our economic competitors.

Today, they are both strategic allies and we are thankful for them but they also happen to compete with us globally. And so we just have to keep in mind that the context is a little different even though the authorities are robust.

Chairman ROYCE. Thank you, Mr. Mancuso.

Here's one more question for you. So we've had a 30 years time- frame here. We've had a number of U.S. Presidents but they've only blocked a total of five CFIUS transactions, two of which hap- pened under this administration here recently.

So given the news yesterday about the White House stopping what would have been the largest deal in tech history, is it fair to conclude that the CFIUS process is evolving toward a stricter re- view process irrespective of potential legislation here by Congress?

Mr. MANCUSO. I will take that question first. I am not going to comment on that specific transaction but I will just comment on the fact that——

Chairman ROYCE. Yes, I remember your caveat coming into the testimony.

Mr. MANCUSO. Yes. The two transactions have been blocked in really as many years, right.

Chairman ROYCE. Right.

Mr. MANCUSO. Actually, now three.

Chairman ROYCE. Right.

Mr. MANCUSO. I think, frankly, the current—the pharma bill largely but not completely would implement current agency practice with CFIUS, okay, and you can quibble about whether or not CFIUS is acting beyond its current authorities but I think it would largely implement that.

Chairman ROYCE. Yes.

Mr. MANCUSO. But I do think the blocking of the transactions suggest that the United States Government, the executive branch, is taking these issues seriously—perhaps in a blunt way, but it's taking these issues more seriously and I think that the U.S. Government needs to take these issues more seriously.

Chairman ROYCE. Thank you, and Mr. Wolf, you wanted to comment on that.

Mr. WOLF. So just to follow up and repeat, the key with all of this is to spend the time and the resources and to have the creativity to identify those emerging technologies of concern that aren't normally looked at in the traditional export control system which we are used to in terms of weapons of mass destruction or traditional military items.

And for this effort to succeed and the former efforts to succeed and the policy objectives in both to be achieved, that, I agree, what really needs to be spent is a lot of very clever thinking, the addition of new resources to the existing system to reach outside the box to identify what those technologies are that are not now controlled but are emerging but should be and to list them and regulate them to the end users and end users of concern.

With respect to the CFIUS question you asked, it all goes down to the deliberate non-definition of national security. National security evolves.

It changes the legislation either the current bill and the—now, the existing statute does not define what that means. It's up to those in charge in order to apply their discretion to what the threat is today.

I believe that the CFIUS system today and before is adequately addressing those and not approving transactions that would leave unresolved national security concerns.

So there can be a guide to what national security means but trying to restrict it or identify or specifically tailor it I don't think would be a good idea because threats and issues evolve.

Chairman ROYCE. Thank you, Mr. Wolf. I appreciate it.

Mr. Engel, ranking member.

Mr. ENGEL. Thank you, Mr. Chairman.

I was happy to join with you a few weeks ago in introducing the Export Control Reform Act in a bipartisan way and, to me, that's been a hallmark, as we've said so many times, of the way this committee operates in a bipartisan way. I wish that more of the committees in this Congress were that way. But I am very pleased that we do.

I am pleased we are following up with this hearing which will help bring members of the committee up to date on our system for controlling the export of dual-use goods and technology, and it isn't something, obviously, we talk about a lot.

But oversight of the export of dual-use items—that is, items that have both military and commercial applications is an important part of our committee's jurisdiction.

In my view, it's just as important as our work regulating the export of military items. A few decades ago, the defense sector nearly always drove the development of high tech, which later ended up on the commercial sector, and today the opposite is often quite true. High tech in the commercial sector is now often a precursor of advanced weapons.

So your bill, Mr. Chairman, will help us take a fresh look at our export control system to bring it up to date with the modern reality of the way these technologies are developed and sold, and it would give us an updated charter that grapples with the global risks of sensitive technology falling into the hands of our adversaries. So this update is long overdue.

As was mentioned, previous law was last revised in 1979 in the depths of the Cold War and is replete with out-of-date provisions that don't reflect national security's provisions today.

It also expired in 2001. It means the authority granting export licenses is no longer based in statute but relies on temporary authority that is now nearly two decades old.

Last year, some 34,000 licenses were processed for exports of sensitive technology, and if you ask me, this isn't something we ought to be doing willy-nilly.

We need a sound updated and permanent statute and that's why, Mr. Chairman, I was so happy and proud to join with you on this.

Let me ask Mr. Wolf and Mr. Mancuso first—each of you managed the export control system while it was under temporary emergency authority and while it was under legal challenge.

So I would like to get you on record. Would you agree that it would be better to have a sound statutory authority for this system?

Mr. MANCUSO. Absolutely, Mr. Engel, and I would go further and say that I think that U.S.' whole of government strategy should be built around export controls, not built around CFIUS.

Mr. ENGEL. Thank you.

Mr. Wolf.

Mr. WOLF. While the existing IEEPA authority is sufficient legal authority for the existing regulations and enforcement there under—I am not denying that—I agree with you that having permanent legal authority in the form of this or a similar bill is very important for a variety of reasons and also to express the will of Congress with respect to a very different world that exists now than existed in 1979. So I agree with the point of your question.

Mr. ENGEL. Thank you.

And let me ask you another one, Mr. Wolf and Mr. Mancuso. Last year, the Export Control Bureau at Commerce and its partners at DOD and State processed 34,000 licenses, and the trend will continue to be upward.

Are the government's resources adequate to handle that volume and make good decisions? I will start with Mr. Mancuso.

Mr. MANCUSO. So just like any enterprise, the government can't do everything everywhere all the time. The number of those licenses—I think BIS has historically been under strain.

I will defer to Kevin on his recent experience. I served for President Bush in that role. But I think as a general proposition, yes, my recollection is that the bureau needs more resources.

But I don't think of resources only in terms of financial resources. I actually think injecting the Bureau of Industry and Security with additional national security acumen and additional connectivity with the rest of the government is important.

I am not suggesting that isn't there. I just think that as an agency that's embedded within a Cabinet department whose principal clients, if you will, or broader commerce I think it's imperative for that agency to remain connected with its national security and foreign policy colleagues to effectively carry out its mandate.

So resources are both financial—would be important—but also in terms of enhanced capability and connectivity with the national security enterprise of the United States.

Mr. ENGEL. Thank you.

Mr. Wolf?

Mr. WOLF. It's great no longer being in government because I could answer your question without being limited to instructions to stick to the budget given.

And, yes, absolutely it's for enforcement both in the United States and outside the United States are critical and the authorities to do it in order to keep the level playing field and to deter those who would violate the regs—for more industry education and outreach, particularly to small and medium-sized businesses I think would be critical, and then going to the point of this hearing, more resources in terms of both money and personnel but creative thinking to identify the types of emerging technologies that aren't traditionally part of the export control system and working with people that aren't traditionally part of the export control world to identify those threats that are novel and not previously considered. And then with respect to resources, that then leads to what I would advocate and always wanted to do on the dual-use side, which is, frankly, a top to bottom list review effort of everything in the very long list of controlled items to see what's there that no longer needs to be—in light of evolving technologies and going back to the emerging point, what isn't there but should be, and that just requires a substantial multi-year effort working with industry, working with experts and the Defense Department, largely, and other parts of the government to figure that out as opposed to the sort of regular process that exists today, which is adequate and good but I think it should be a lot more robust and aggressive.

Mr. ENGEL. Thank you.

And Ambassador Larson, I have one quick one for you. Given your experience at State, are the budget and staff cutbacks that we are seeing at State having a negative effect on the department?

Ambassador LARSON. I haven't worked there for 12 years but my judgment is that it's very hard for the State Department to do the missions that it's been asked to do with such a tight budget situation, certainly in the areas I was responsible for in economics. I think that's true.

Mr. ENGEL. Thank you. Thank you, Mr. Chairman.

Chairman ROYCE. Thank you, Mr. Engel.

We go to Mr. Chris Smith of New Jersey.

Mr. SMITH. Thank you very much, Mr. Chairman. I want to thank our witnesses for their insight and recommendations.

Mr. Chairman, I am very concerned by reports that U.S. companies are selling equipment and technology that is being used by the Chinese Government in its ubiquitous surveillance and detention program, including the targeting of Uighur Muslim ethnic minority persons in western China.

Some estimates suggest that something like 500,000—some put it much higher—Uighurs are being detained in political education centers, which are really just detention centers.

This is a staggering figure. Included in the crackdown are family members of Voice of America, Uighur-language broadcasters.

Chinese police are gathering and storing DNA samples, fingerprints, iris scans, and blood types, and other biometric data from all Uighurs between the ages of 12 and 65.

Human Rights Watch identified a Massachusetts-based company, Thermo Fisher Scientific, as supplying the Chinese Government with DNA sequencers.

Other companies are providing surveillance cameras or software for facial recognition equipment.

Would you say that United States law bars U.S. companies from exporting technology that aids in the crackdown of the Uighurs?

To me, that would seem clear. The 1978 amendment to Section 502(b) of the Foreign Assistance Act of 1961 states that export licenses may not be issued under the Export Administration Act of '69 for the export of crime control and detection instruments and equipment to a country, the government of which engages in a consistent pattern of gross violations of internationally recognized human rights, unless the President certifies in writing to the Speaker of the House and the chairman of the Committee on Foreign Affairs and the Senate Foreign Relations that extraordinary circumstances exist warranting provision of such assistance and the issuing of such a license.

We've checked with the House Foreign Affairs Committee and Speaker's office and neither have received a certification for this sale of detection and surveillance equipment to China.

So the question is: Are companies allowed to export that, especially now that we know that it's being used against the Uighurs?

Are you aware of any company selling equipment and technology that China is using for its massive police state surveillance efforts, and how can U.S. companies sell technology and equipment that is being used for these purposes?

Is that a problem that the Commerce and the State Departments are not policing this area very well? Is it a matter of negligence, or is the problem with the law and does that law have to be rewritten in a world where DNA sequencers, biometric data gathering, and the use of artificial intelligence for surveillance is now becoming commonplace?

Ambassador.

Ambassador LARSON. Well, thank you, Mr. Smith. I would like to defer to the two colleagues who actually ran export controls.

Mr. SMITH. That's great.

Mr. WOLF. Sure. So most of this discussion today is about national security controls. But foreign policy controls, crime controls, which includes human rights issues that you raised, are very much a part of——

Mr. SMITH. If I could interrupt.

Mr. WOLF. Yes.

Mr. SMITH. I would always say that human rights violations, particularly on such a massive scale, absolutely rise to the level of a national security issue for the United States.

Mr. WOLF. Okay. Fair point. Fair point. I often—but in any event, it covers both, either national security, foreign policy, human rights, however defined.

And the key to the point of your question is with respect to the technology, and I don't know the facts involved, is whether the items of concern are listed on the commerce control list and there are long lists of items that are controlled for crime control—CC reasons—such as fingerprint equipment and things like that that are controlled for exactly the reasons that you just described.

With respect to the facts that you're dealing with, the question would be whether they are on the list now and, if not, should they be or if there are reasons where they're not.

Again, I don't know but that would be the question to ask and to work with BIS, and even to the extent that it's not the equipment at issue but the act of the foreign parties that are of national security or foreign policy concern, then BIS and the EAR have the authority to list particular entities which could result in the prohibition on the export of any items—coffee cups, biometric equipment, et cetera—for the sake of exerting pressure on companies outside the U.S. or entities from engaging in bad acts, and that's called the entity-less process and it's a tool that BIS has to address issues such as along the lines that you describe to the extent that listing the equipment for control would not achieve the objectives sought.

Mr. SMITH. Thank you.

Mr. MANCUSO. Congressman Smith, my experience at BIS has been, you know, somewhat dated but I will answer your question.

The authority exists to stop those kinds of items. In the last decade, of course, the technology, I believe, in this area in particular has really developed.

But during my time at BIS we took this very seriously. Some of those items we in fact interdicted but some of these items were essentially dual use so we did not.

But I agree with the premise of your question, which is that this is an area that the export control regime should look at and consider against U.S. policy objectives.

So the legal authority is there and it's a policy question about whether it's done on any given basis.

Mr. SMITH. Thank you so much.

Mr. MANCUSO. Thank you.

Chairman ROYCE. Thank you.

Mr. Brad Sherman of California.

Mr. SHERMAN. As others have noticed, we are operating for the last quarter century under an expired dual-use export statute—the Export Administration Act.

Its regulations are kept in force under IEEPA. This is not regular order. This is not the rule of law as it is supposed to be carried out.

It has worked, more or less. This is a critical area of jurisdiction for this committee and we've allowed the executive branch to run the policy.

We've got to change that, of course, so that's why I commend Chairman Royce and Ranking Member Engel for introducing 5054—that's H.R. 5054—to update the statute in this area.

This is not the first attempt. There have been many attempts over the years. About a decade ago, we faced a bit of a crisis because DDTC in the State Department was taking many, many months to process applications and tens of thousands of applications were languishing.

Pressure by this committee and the subcommittee that the chairman chaired and then I chaired and then he chaired again at least pushed the administration to solve that problem.

The major effect of legislation in this area was to move satellites from the munitions list back onto the commerce list. There are many who believe that the maximum national security can be achieved by putting the maximum controls on the maximum number of items.

This may not be the case. When we don't export goods we weaken our industrial base, setting back the money that's available to develop the weapons and technologies of the future.

When we don't sell something, the buyer goes somewhere else and strengthens the industrial base of a country willing to sell to them and perhaps willing to sell to an even worse country.

And so I've been a proponent of having a taller fence around a smaller field and that is to figure out what we are going to control and control it very well.

I should point out that China blames our technology controls for the enormous trade deficit. That is just their attempt to lie about the real reasons for the enormous trade deficit.

Let's see. One area that I would like to address to the witnesses—believe it or not, I have a question in here, which is new for me—is should we make the decisions based—especially at the Commerce—well, does Commerce look at the impacts the technology transfer will have not just on the narrow security issue of whether that particular item will be misused in a way that hurts our security but from an employment standpoint, from an industrial base standpoint?

Do we take a look at how the transfer of that technology will lead to the outsourcing of whole areas of production?

So, Ambassador, I will start with you. Does Commerce take a look at the industrial base and especially the jobs issues?

Ambassador LARSON. Thank you, Mr. Sherman. If I may, because my expertise doesn't lie primarily in the Commerce Depart‐ ment——

Mr. SHERMAN. Then I will go to Mr. Wolf.

Ambassador LARSON [continuing]. I would like to answer the question in a broader frame. Is that all right or should I just turn——

Mr. SHERMAN. Why don't we go to the people who will answer it their own way?

Ambassador LARSON. That's fine.

Mr. WOLF. Sure. I am not of the view of those who subscribe to there should be a balance between national security and jobs or economic security. National security is paramount and all decisions are to——

Mr. SHERMAN. Yes. I am asking here are there times where we should say no, not because that one item could hurt our national security but because the export of that particular technology will allow a competitor to enter a whole new field that previously had been dependent on U.S. technology. I am not saying say yes to cre‐ ate jobs. I am saying are there times we should say no to protect jobs.

Mr. WOLF. That variable is not a factor in what the Commerce Department considers when deciding whether to approve or deny an individual license. It's if that technology would create a national security threat you approve—you deny it or mitigate it——

Mr. SHERMAN. So if there's a crown jewel that supports tens of thousands of jobs in America because we have that technology, Commerce may allow it to be exported?

Mr. Mancuso.

Mr. MANCUSO. So, Congressman Sherman, I would take the ap‐ proach no, we wouldn't because we don't balance national security against jobs. We certainly balance——

Mr. SHERMAN. I think you're making the same mistake on the question.

Mr. MANCUSO. No, actually——

Mr. SHERMAN. Do we say no, you can't export that item even it may be consistent with national security, but because the export of that item means a whole industry is being exported.

Mr. MANCUSO. I think it's important to keep in mind the two risks you identified—the transaction risk and systemic risk—this industrial base issue.

I think with respect to certain crown jewels where the actual law—national security loss in any given transaction—an export of the crown jewel, to use your example—I would take the position we don't balance that. If it's a crown jewel, it's a crown jewel.

On the other hand, we have to be very discerning about what is a crown jewel because there are many technologies that might be sensitive but are not crown jewels and with respect to those econo‐ mies of scale matter.

Semi—lower-grade semiconductors are a good example of why we export them around the world and why it's important to export those around the world because the U.S. has an interest in protecting crown jewels but has no interest in creating protected foreign markets.

Mr. SHERMAN. I've gone over time. I yield back.

Mr. MANCUSO. Has no interest in protecting—creating protected foreign markets if it's not advancing a U.S. national security interest.

Chairman ROYCE. We go to Mr. Ted Yoho of Florida.

Mr. YOHO. Thank you, Mr. Chairman, and I appreciate you guys being here. I could sit here all day and talk to you guys about this stuff because I think it's so important.

Mr. Mancuso, you brought up that the U.S. Government should build its policies around export controls, not CFIUS. Did I hear that right?

Mr. MANCUSO. Yes, and what I meant by that, Congressman, is that export controls is a big piece. Obviously, CFIUS plays a very important role. But we have to think of complementary——

Mr. YOHO. That's what I want to—they need—that can't be and/or.

Mr. MANCUSO. They can't be separate. It's not and/or. It's both. Mr. YOHO. They've got to be together. You know, we were talking about intellectual properties and we just came back from a trip to Thailand and they were talking about the special 311 report on IPRs and how Thailand is on the watch list. But they're doing the things necessary to make sure that they protect our IPRs of our entrepreneurs.

We are talking about intellectual property and it seems to rotate more around national security interests or the Broadcom or Qualcomm deal that the President stepped in, and as Chairman Royce brought up, the current administration did step in twice of the five times that were done in a period of years.

And if you have an aggressive executive office that's well but we need to make sure that the rules are in place and I bring up—it's not just the intellectual property on a national security or with semiconductors, things like that.

I was in a meeting yesterday where our researchers from our land grants were working with biogenomes with plants and he says, "I am an adjunct professor in China because they pay me three times what I am paying here."

And what they're doing is they're taking our intellectual property in research and development in the ag science fields, taking them over there and it's not benefiting us.

They're benefiting from our beginning research and I think this too is something that should be looked at different than we do now.

And we've seen this over and over again. We saw the story up in Iowa where the Chinese operatives were stealing GMO corn, taking it over there and, again, it's a competitive advantage that they will get over us.

So with that, is anybody looking at the biosciences? Before you answer that, the Chinese Government plans to force $9 billion into the National Precision Medicine Initiative before 2030.

That's a lot of money and it's similar—the U.S. has only put in $215 million to their $9 billion and it's clear that they're going to get the competitive advantage.

And then one has to wonder why is China building such a large pool. Right now, they have 30 percent of the world's genomics that they control and I can see this as a weapon in the future, you know, when you can start manipulating genes against a population and, again, we've had our medical researchers say that they'll start drug trials. They run out of money here. China picks it up and finishes it.

So this drug that we put the initial research into it gets developed with an Asian population and it may not work the same in a Western population.

And so are we looking at those as strong as we are on radars and semiconductors, in your experience? And that's for all of you.

Mr. MANCUSO. So, Congressman, export controls and CFIUS are complementary but they're only two instruments we have to counter some of the things.

So things like industrial espionage, frankly, the purposeful stealing of technologies export controls is likely not going to catch.

We need other instruments for that, and other parts of the government have been working on that. I can't tell you that my information is up to date what the progress of those efforts are.

But if the premise of your question that we should be watching that is what—if that's what it is, I agree with it. So that's when I—

—

Mr. YOHO. Well, let me narrow that down. Do we have the controls in place now to protect all the sciences that we are doing? Are we mainly just focused on the telecommunications and the semiconductors?

Mr. MANCUSO. This goes to—and then I will pass it over to Kevin—we have the authorities to control all of that.

The government as a whole needs to and regularly does discuss, you know, views about what technology should be controlled but whether those specific technologies are controlled.

Certainly, some radars are controlled. Certainly some therapies are controlled. But I am not quite sure if all of them, at least the ones that you're thinking about are.

Mr. YOHO. I think that's something we need to weigh in and you brought up. Countries not individuals today are spying and they've always done that and they're always going to do that.

But what we are seeing is a different geopolitics today than we had 15, 20 years ago. We have a very aggressive China going after things by hook and crook and it's not just the individual out there doing the espionage. It's a country and that country is taking that stuff from us.

Mr. Wolf, if you want to weigh in, in 5 seconds.

Mr. WOLF. No, export controls are not the solution to all those issues. They're not good for industrial policy. They're not good for economic espionage or IP theft or funding issues or R&D advantages.

So all of those things that you mentioned are very important. But the EAR, the Export Administration Regulations, are probably not the best place to try to address them, given the national security and foreign policy focus of them.

Mr. YOHO. I thank you for your time and I would like to follow up with you later.

Mr. WOLF. Sure.

Mr. YOHO. Mr. Chairman.

Chairman ROYCE. Thank you. Thank you, Mr. Yoho.

We go now to Mr. Albio Sires of New Jersey.

Mr. SIRES. Thank you, Mr. Chairman, and thank you for the panel that's here today.

And I just want to follow up on my good friend from Florida on some of the things that he said. I know the title of this hearing today, but I really want to get it down to basics so I can understand some things.

First thing, I remember a few years ago with solar panels—we developed the panels—energy. China gets it and then they dump the solar panels on us.

I represent New Jersey. I constantly hear from the pharmaceutical industry how Canada dumps things in America, some of the things that we develop here.

Now we have India. Now South America is getting into the act. I know that—I keep hearing that we have the authority to control these things—these imports.

How does that happen? How do we develop the energy—the solar panel energy, goes away from here, comes back here. Don't we have any kind of control on that stuff?

And how, if we develop these medicines in the pharmaceutical industry and we have places like Canada, which is supposed to be our best trading partner, dump the stuff here. I meant, to me, I am missing something.

And I know Mr. Wolf, I hear you going back and forth. Sometimes you talk too fast for me. Maybe I'm stupid this morning.

But, you know, I would just like to get some sort of a response.

Ambassador LARSON. Well, I thought—yes. Congressman, maybe I could begin to address some of your very good questions.

You know, I think all of us have emphasized the fact that we need to use a multiplicity of tools. We can't just use one tool.

CFIUS has a role to play. The Export Administration Act and the new legislation that's been introduced has a role to play on export controls.

A lot of the problems that you're raising are ones that have to be addressed through traditional trade policy measures—things that are led by the U.S. Trade Representative's office but where the White House, State Department, Commerce Department play important roles.

Now, you know, solar panels—there's been a decision that's been taken under the authority of Section 201 of the Trade Act.

Some of the issues related to pharmaceutical products also have been a key concern. We heard earlier about some of the concerns about intellectual property theft in Thailand and measures to get Thailand to do a better job of protecting against those things.

There is a very focused effort—very quickly—on China and the Section 301 investigation that is currently underway to address those practices.

So those are other tools that will address some of the concerns that you're talking about, sir.

Mr. SIRES. I just don't know if we have the ability to get some of these countries to stop doing these things. I mean, what controls do we have?

I mean, Thailand, for example, they don't have much of an economy. I mean, do we want them to stop? How do we do that?

I am sorry, Mr. Mancuso?

Mr. MANCUSO. So I actually think, Congressman, it's a very good question. The U.S. Government has different agencies that have those responsibilities.

I think the world in which we—I mean, there are lots of problems. We can talk Thailand. We can talk China. But I think they're all different.

The U.S. Government has the capability and has the authority to do those things. But with respect to certain—both economic partners and strategic competitors like China, I think our game has to be better. It has to be more coordinated.

And so it's a legitimate question for Congress to ask in a specific way vis-a-vis this threat—are we configured—are we resourced to address this threat, and those are important questions to ask.

I wish I had better answers. We can do it. I am not sure we are doing it well against the numbers—the various threats that we are——

Mr. SIRES. Can somebody address the pharmaceutical industry? Because that is very important to my state.

Mr. WOLF. Yes, but not in the Export Administration Regulations. The subject of this bill and the regulations at issue couldn't solve your problem but many other areas like 201, 301—yeah. No, I mean, it's a legitimate issue but it's not the subject or capable of being addressed by the Export Administration Regulations, which are focused on more traditional national security and foreign policy issues of the threat as opposed to the economic considerations at issue behind your question. These regulations don't get to that point.

Mr. SIRES. Right. I get it but do you have any regulations that get to it? Not you. How about——

Ambassador LARSON. Well, I think the key——

Mr. SIRES. I am specifically talking about Canada and the United States. Let me put it this way.

Ambassador LARSON. Well, and so on Canada and the United States I think you raised an issue that must be at the heart of the NAFTA renegotiations that are underway right now and, certainly, the broad question of protection of intellectual property rights of companies like pharmaceutical companies that invest billions of dollars in developing new products lie at the heart of most of the trade negotiations that USTR leads on behalf of our Government.

Mr. SIRES. Well, I just want to thank you.

Thank you, Chairman.

Mr. YOHO [presiding]. Thank you for the questions.

Next, we'll go to Ann Wagner from Missouri.

Mrs. WAGNER. Thank you, Mr. Chairman, for hosting this important hearing.

This issue is important to my district, as China has been looking to expand its footprint in the Midwest. Representatives from the Chinese consulate in Chicago spent the past year networking with Midwestern government offices including a stop in my district office and they stated that, and I quote, "Suspicion of Chinese foreign direct investment and excessive national security reviews would be bad for the bilateral relationship."

However, I was quick to remind them that failing to properly control our exports would be bad for America.

I am committed to working with the committee to re-evaluate our export control regime to ensure that it is up to the challenge. And I thank you.

Mr. Mancuso, I appreciate your insights on the Foreign Investment Risk Review Modernization Act, or FIRRMA. You noted that the bill encourages heightened engagement with our allies.

The more closely we coordinate with foreign partners, the better our own export control regime will work. There is an opportunity here to expand the list of countries that participate in multilateral export control regimes, especially in Asia.

For example, the U.S. has strong ties with Singapore and Malaysia, which have struggled to prevent controlled goods from making their way into North Korea and China.

What, sir, can Congress do to help these countries become productive partners in our export control system?

Mr. MANCUSO. Good morning, Congresswoman. So I will do my best to answer that question.

First things first. I do think international trade and investment—foreign direct investment in most cases is overwhelmingly positive, including with respect to China.

But I think we have to be very sober about those areas where it's not. This is true for foreign investment. This is true for tech transfer export controls.

In terms of the things this—our Government should do with respect to our partners and allies around the world, I would distinguish between treaty partners and treaty allies and partners.

They're all important. We value their relationships. They all contribute something. But treaty allies, I think, are special.

With respect to those, I think the United States should engage in this kind of diplomacy to ensure that people—our colleagues understand our perspective. They may disagree and they're entitled to disagree. They're sovereign nations.

But they should understand our perspective of why technology transfer is important and why the regulation of certain foreign investment is important.

I would just point out in response that that some of our NATO allies are now considering either implementing or upgrading their CFIUS-like regimes.

I think, if done well, that is a good thing. I think it is in the U.S. interests that our treaty partners have resilient economies and they have economies that support their national security interests as well, which tend to coincide with ours.

Mrs. WAGNER. Both the United States and China are deeply aware that economic and national security can't be separated, as we've stated here today at the hearing.

Ambassador Larson, I am curious about how China might respond to FIRRMA. Can you give us a status update on Beijing's foreign investment law?

Also, what might the Chinese version of CFIUS look like and how would it affect our bilateral relationship?

Ambassador LARSON. Well, thank you for the question.

First of all, I've had a lot of conversations with the Chinese when I was in government and the role I have now, and the complaints about CFIUS and about export controls are sort of a persistent theme.

And I've been a pretty strong, a very strong defender, actually, that the way that our Government in the United States has implemented CFIUS has been very targeted and has focused on those transactions that could present a threat to national security.

And I will continue to take that position and I think that should be a position that will be embodied in the reforms that are contemplated in FIRRMA.

China does have a national security law that affects investment in China right now. I don't think it is implemented in as sophisticated way as CFIUS is administered.

I think that it will be important when some of our Western allies implement national security-based investment laws as well because

I think having a relatively common approach, whether it's on export controls or on inward investment controls, is a strong point for us. When we can do that with our major allies, that's important. I think we are just going to have a very candid set of conversa- tions with China that start from the point that we understand that a two-way investment is good for both of our economies.

We understand that we do depend on each other's economies. But we will take the steps that we need to take to ensure that investment is not permitted or acquisitions are not permitted that impair our national security.

So I think it's a time where very candid conversations with China on the nature of our economic relationship—trade and investment—are going to be required to work out the problems that we have in the relationship.

Mrs. WAGNER. Thank you very much. My time has expired.

Mr. Chairman, I will submit the rest of my questions for the record. Thank you.

Chairman ROYCE [presiding]. I thank the gentlelady.

Tom Garrett of Virginia.

Mr. GARRETT. Thank you, Mr. Chairman, and I would tip my hat, in his absence, to Senator Cornyn for working on this important legislation and to the chairman and ranking member of this committee.

And I would point to a quote from someone I don't quote that often, Vladimir Lenin, who said, "We will hang the capitalists with the rope that they sell us," and I would submit that, anecdotally, as a young Army officer I heard a story of Q36 and Q37 Firefinder radars finding their way to China during the Clinton administration only to have American military Warrant Officers sent to help the Chinese put them back together I presume to reverse engineer them and those of us who knew what that counter battery radar allowed us to do wondered how the hell they got to China.

Now, it's anecdotal. It's hearsay, as I would say in a later career. But I know this stuff happens. It blows my mind that Gen3 GPS signals were given to our enemies under President Clinton and have literally been used at the very least to take the lives of our allies.

And I understand that there was much made about the transfer from the NTIA to ICANN of controls over the internet and some of it was hyperbolic and overstated but some of it wasn't, and I wonder what the heck we are doing.

So let me ask about FIRRMA and CFIUS as it relates to EB-5 visas. Would the FIRRMA Act extend into the realm of the granting of EB-5 visas?

Mr. Mancuso.

Mr. MANCUSO. Congressman, I don't think so. I would be surprised if they would. I don't know.

Mr. GARRETT. Does anybody at this table believe that that's not the case? I believe that that's the case, that you're correct.

Mr. WOLF. It does not. But in the export control system, there are prohibitions on what are called deemed exports, which are the released technologies to foreign persons in the United States regardless of the visa or other reasons they're——

Mr. GARRETT. All right. Mr. Wolf, with all due respect, and I mean that——

Mr. WOLF. Yes.

Mr. GARRETT [continuing]. I got a finite amount of time.

Mr. WOLF. Okay.

Mr. GARRETT. But so it doesn't.

Mr. WOLF. So no, but yes.

Mr. GARRETT. And so might it make sense to extend some sort of congressional oversight and review to the EB-5 visa issuance process, Mr. Larson?

Ambassador LARSON. I think that Congress can and should look at all things that it thinks could be important to——

Mr. GARRETT. And do you think it could be important to make sure that we are giving EB-5 visas to the right people who might not have dual-source technology at their fingertips by virtue of a permanent residence in the United States and a business that essentially manufactures what might be sensitive technology? Yes or no, please.

Ambassador LARSON. I—if I were in the State Department I would not want to give a visa to someone that was coming to the United States for the purpose of stealing technology.

Mr. GARRETT. So when the Washington Post—the Washington Post, noted conservative-leaning paper, right—that's tongue in cheek—says that Virginia Governor Terry McAuliffe garnered special privilege in receiving EB-5 visas through the Department of Homeland Security under the Obama administration, we know that he lined his pockets.

We know that GreenTech Automotive is now defunct and that the taxpayers of the state of Mississippi have lost millions of dollars.

But to the extent that things like lithium ion batteries, which is undergird by the Chinese monopolization of the global cobalt markets, et cetera, can have dual uses, would not selling permanent residence to the United States potentially compromise technology that might be that proverbial rope that Lenin says they will buy from us to use to hang us, Mr. Mancuso?

Mr. MANCUSO. The answer is that's—let me answer this differently. I don't think we should—I think citizenship is special. Citizenship goes to how you feel about your country and your commitment to your country.

This is an existing program. I think it's certainly something that this Congress could look at as part of a broader view of how we think about the U.S.' engagement with the rest of the world.

Mr. GARRETT. Again—and again, sincerely thank you all for being here. I intend absolutely no disrespect. I have a finite amount of time.

EB-5 visas grant not citizenship but permanent residence under green card status for people who invest $500,000 in under developed areas or $1 million in developed areas of the United States to engage in the discourse of commerce.

However, in 2014 I believe we granted just over 10,000 EB-5 visas. I am not that good at math but 85 percent of them, or north of 8,500, were to Chinese nationals to engage in commerce on American soil wherein, I would presume, they would have lower barriers to entry as it related to obtaining technology that might have dual uses.

Mr. Wolf, you're nodding.

Mr. WOLF. Yes, I agree you have a legitimate issue with that exact point for that reason. Just because they become a citizen through that process that their motives with respect to acquisition of dual-use technology should be part of the process.

Mr. GARRETT. And so that's something that you gentlemen would concur. And, again, I am out of time but I am going to ask real quickly, Mr. Chair, that we might ought to review as well in conjunction with CFIUS and the actual sending overseas of technology itself.

Mr. MANCUSO. Absolutely.

Mr. GARRETT. Thank you. Thank you, Mr. Chairman.

Chairman ROYCE. Thank you very much, Tom.

Let me just conclude our hearing here by thanking all three of our members of this panel for coming and testifying and also for giving us your insights on the pending legislation, and if none of you would mind, we'll, of course, have some additional questions, as we move forward.

So thank you very much, and we stand adjourned.

[Whereupon, at 11:26 a.m., the committee was adjourned.]

APPENDIX

Material Submitted for the Record

FULL COMMITTEE HEARING NOTICE
COMMITTEE ON FOREIGN AFFAIRS
U.S. HOUSE OF REPRESENTATIVES
WASHINGTON, DC 20515-6128

Edward R. Royce (R-CA), Chairman

March 14, 2018

TO: MEMBERS OF THE COMMITTEE ON FOREIGN AFFAIRS

You are respectfully requested to attend an OPEN hearing of the Committee on Foreign Affairs to be held in Room 2172 of the Rayburn House Office Building (and available live on the Committee website at http://www.ForeignAffairs.house.gov):

DATE: Wednesday, March 14, 2018

TIME: 10:00 a.m.

SUBJECT: Modernizing Export Controls: Protecting Cutting-Edge Technology and U.S. National Security

WITNESSES: The Honorable Mario Mancuso
                    Partner
                    Kirkland and Ellis, LLP
                    (*Former Undersecretary for Industry and Security, U.S. Department of Commerce*)

                    The Honorable Alan Larson
                    Senior International Policy Advisor
                    Covington and Burling, LLP
                    (*Former Undersecretary for Economic, Business, and Agricultural Affairs, U.S. Department of State*)

                    The Honorable Kevin Wolf
                    Partner
                    Akin Gump Strauss Hauer and Feld, LLP
                    (*Former Assistant Secretary for Export Administration, Bureau of Industry and Security, U.S. Department of Commerce*)

By Direction of the Chairman

COMMITTEE ON FOREIGN AFFAIRS
MINUTES OF FULL COMMITTEE HEARING

Day _**Wednesday**_ Date _**03/14/2018**_ Room _**2172**_

Starting Time _**10:09 a.m.**_ Ending Time _**11:26 a.m.**_

Recesses _**0**_ (___to___) (___to___) (___to___) (___to___) (___to___) (___to___)

Presiding Member(s)
Chairman Edward R. Royce
Representative Ted Yoho

Check all of the following that apply:

Open Session ☑
Executive (closed) Session ☐
Televised ☑

Electronically Recorded (taped) ☑
Stenographic Record ☑

TITLE OF HEARING:

Modernzing Export Controls: Protecting Cutting Edge Technology and U.S. National Security

COMMITTEE MEMBERS PRESENT:

See attached.

NON-COMMITTEE MEMBERS PRESENT:

N/A

HEARING WITNESSES: Same as meeting notice attached? Yes ☑ No ☐
(If "no", please list below and include title, agency, department, or organization.)

STATEMENTS FOR THE RECORD: *(List any statements submitted for the record.)*

QFR - Representatives Kinzinger and Wagner
SFR - Representative Connolly

TIME SCHEDULED TO RECONVENE _______
or
TIME ADJOURNED _**11:26 a.m.**_

____
Full Committee Hearing Coordinator

HOUSE COMMITTEE ON FOREIGN AFFAIRS

FULL COMMITTEE HEARING

PRESENT	MEMBER
X	Edward R. Royce, CA
X	Christopher H. Smith, NJ
	Ileana Ros-Lehtinen, FL
	Dana Rohrabacher, CA
X	Steve Chabot, OH
X	Joe Wilson, SC
X	Michael T. McCaul, TX
X	Ted Poe, TX
X	Darrell Issa, CA
	Tom Marino, PA
X	Mo Brooks, AL
	Paul Cook, CA
X	Scott Perry, PA
X	Ron DeSantis, FL
	Mark Meadows, NC
X	Ted Yoho, FL
	Adam Kinzinger, IL
X	Lee Zeldin, NY
X	Dan Donovan, NY
	James F. Sensenbrenner, Jr., WI
X	Ann Wagner, MO
	Brian J. Mast, FL
X	Brian K. Fitzpatrick, PA
	Francis Rooney, FL
X	Thomas A. Garrett, Jr., VA
	John Curtis, UT

PRESENT	MEMBER
X	Eliot L. Engel, NY
X	Brad Sherman, CA
	Gregory W. Meeks, NY
X	Albio Sires, NJ
X	Gerald E. Connolly, VA
	Theodore E. Deutch, FL
	Karen Bass, CA
	William Keating, MA
	David Cicilline, RI
X	Ami Bera, CA
	Lois Frankel, FL
	Tulsi Gabbard, HI
	Joaquin Castro, TX
X	Robin Kelly, IL
	Brendan Boyle, PA
	Dina Titus, NV
	Norma Torres, CA
X	Brad Schneider, IL
	Tom Suozzi, NY
	Adriano Espaillat, NY
	Ted Lieu, CA

Statement for the Record
Submitted by Mr. Connolly of Virginia

The U.S. export control regime should strike a careful balance between supporting the health and competitiveness of U.S. high-technology industries and protecting U.S. national security. The current system is failing to maintain that equilibrium and modernization is long overdue. The Department of Commerce has relied on the President's emergency economic authority to maintain its export control regulations for more than two decades. Legal challenges abound leaving the regime subject to wild fluctuations in implementation. It is clear that the system would benefit from a more permanent statutory framework. At the same time, our adversaries, particularly China, are increasing their efforts to acquire critical American technologies. Reforms to modernize the export control system must address these national security threats.

The U.S. export control system is designed to protect U.S. national security by regulating the export of defense items, goods and technology used for both civilian and military applications ("dual-use" exports), and inputs for nuclear, chemical, and biological weapons. Both the regulation and enforcement of the current regime involve robust interagency cooperation among the main U.S. export control agencies, namely the Departments of Commerce, State, and Treasury. Under the current system, transferring controlled technology requires a license, approved agreement, exception, or exemption.

The Export Administration Act of 1979 (EAA) provided the statutory authority underpinning the dual-use export controls. However, that statute expired in 1994, and with the exception of one incremental extension in 2000, the export licensing system has had to rely on a presidential emergency declaration and the invocation of the International Emergency Economic Powers Act (IEEPA) in order to maintain the current system. In addition, adversaries like China have aggressively pursued sensitive U.S. technologies by increasing foreign investment in knowledge-intensive, high-technology sectors. Chinese investment in the United States totaled more than $46 billion in 2016 alone.

Chairman Royce and Ranking Member Engel have introduced H.R. 5040, the Export Control Reform Act of 2018, which would repeal the lapsed Export Administration Act of 1979 and replace it with a permanent statutory authority to better regulate commercial and military products licensed by the Department of Commerce. When I was in the private sector, I had to take cumbersome compliance courses to understand the legal complexities of this system. Enacting a permanent statutory basis for our export control system will help U.S. companies by stabilizing administration of the controls and protecting their sensitive technologies from unauthorized transfer.

I am pleased that this Committee is prioritizing export control reform and examining the issues related to revamping our export control regime. I look forward to hearing from our witnesses regarding how we can strike the necessary balance between supporting U.S. high-technology companies and protecting U.S. national security by keeping sensitive technologies out of the hands of those who would do us harm.

Questions for the Record from Rep. Adam Kinzinger
Modernizing Export Controls: Protecting Cutting-Edge Technology and U.S. National Security
March 14, 2018

Question

This question is for Mr. Wolf and Mr. Mancuso, regarding the Bureau of Industry and Security's role in the Excess Defense Articles Program. One of the main roles of BIS is to protect the American industrial base. How does the BIS determine what is in the best interest of the industrial base? What if two American parties differ on whether a proposed EDA transfer is good for the industrial base? How does BIS make that determination? Further, what transparency obligations must BIS meet—either statutory or regulatory—to ensure that the transfers are in the best interest of the American taxpayer? What do you think could be improved with respect to transparency at BIS?

Answer

Mr. Wolf's Response:

The Defense Security Cooperation Agency (DSCA) is responsible for administering EDA. Section 516(b)(1)(e) of the Foreign Assistance Act states that EDA transfers shall not adversely impact the U.S. national technology and industrial base, nor reduce the opportunities of U.S. industry to sell new or used equipment to the proposed recipient. In accordance with Executive Order 12163, as amended, the Director of DSCA makes the determination on the impact to industry. BIS has only an informal advisory role to DSCA. Please check with BIS to be certain, but I do not recall any formal or informal arrangements between BIS and DSCA on the topic. That is, I do not believe there are any relevant memoranda of understanding or regulations to address your question. As I recall, BIS would give its informal opinions, but DSCA was responsible for the decision. This was not a program I was involved with during my tenure, so I will have to defer to BIS for a more fulsome answer.

Mr. Mancuso's Response:

Through participation in various programs and activities, including conducting U.S. industrial base surveys and assessments, involvement with CFIUS reviews, and providing the Department of Defense with input on implications of proposed Excess Defense Article ("EDA") transfers, BIS exercises its responsibilities to protect the U.S. defense industrial base. Where there is a possibility that an EDA transfer will have an adverse impact on U.S. military readiness or affect a U.S. industry initiative to market similar products to a country to which the transfer is destined, BIS can provide an adverse recommendation on the transfer to the Director of the Defense Security Cooperation Agency ("DSCA"), which is responsible for administering the EDA program. With respect to transparency, EDA transfer data is available to the general public at DSCA's website.

Questions for the Record from Rep. Ann Wagner
Modernizing Export Controls: Protecting Cutting-Edge Technology and U.S. National Security
March 14, 2018

<u>Question</u>

Mr. Wolf, I know that the Department of Commerce's Bureau of Industry and Security places a premium on private-public partnerships. Experts told us that the enforcement side relies on contacts in the private sector, much like regular police officers rely on their relationships with people in the community. The *Export Control Reform Act* would encourage further public-private collaboration. What is the most effective way Commerce can enhance public-private relationships?

<u>Answer</u>

As I mentioned in my testimony, export controls should not "balance" national security concerns with economic concerns. National security concerns are not to be traded off for something else in a particular transaction. Rather, they should be properly calibrated, tailored controls to avoid collateral economic costs, unnecessary regulatory burdens, and misallocation of federal resources. It is at this point where the interaction with industry occurs – and the goal is to ensure maximum compliance in the least regulatory burdensome way possible. The following are examples of ways such goals can be accomplished:

1. Massive amounts of education and outreach. There can never be enough training in the rules, which are inherently complex and always impose some degree of burden. With regular outreach, such as through conferences, seminars, and direct company visits, industry can learn directly from the government regularly how the controls work. And the government officials can hear directly from industry what is hard for it to understand. BIS is unique among the export control agencies in that it has a dedicated office of education and outreach to do exactly this. The amount of work it can do is a direct function of the resources available to it to hire trained staff.

There are many other tools that can be used in addition to such traditional efforts. For example, when I was Assistant Secretary, I held almost every Wednesday an open conference call where I would give the public updates on developments with the rules and then would answer every and any question the participants would have about the rules. So, every week, anyone in industry would have direct access to the Assistant Secretary and get answers to everyone's stated questions about the export control rules. This obviously was of benefit to industry, but we also benefited from the types of questions asked. It showed us what was not clear to industry and gave us a good sense for the types of improvements we needed to make to the regulations. We also created many online decision trees for industry to use to help it work through particularly complex regulatory provisions. We recorded seminars on particular provisions and made them available for free. These and other tools created a constant feedback loop with industry. This lead to better controls – more compliance, less confusion. Finally, such outreach is particularly important for small- and medium-sized US companies because they do not generally have the large compliance staff larger companies do. They need more help generally.

2. Unless absolutely necessary, publish rule changes as proposed, sometimes more than once, to get industry input. That is, avoid publish rules for the first time as final rules. Government officials are smart, but they can never really know how a rule will be understood until it is tested by the regulated community. Industry will know its products better and, if the government is clear about the goals to be achieved, often recommend reasonable drafting edits to make the rules more clear and effective.

3. Maintain an active technical advisory committee (TAC) system. The TACS, which are made up of industry experts, are an excellent source of information of commercialization of listed technologies and the emergence of new technologies of concern. TAC members work directly with government officials to provide technical expertise, both internally and with the multilateral regimes. TAC members do such work for free, so they should be thanked regularly for their contributions.

4. Enforcement officials can be a significant source of training for industry during their site visits. Their primary role is to investigate and enforce the rules, of course, but, in the course of doing so, they have significant contact with industry and can be a valuable source of compliance advice.

5. We created a routine of having compliance program officials visit companies to help them improve their compliance programs. Such efforts are important to the goal as well. BIS cannot be there for every transaction, but assisting companies in how set up procedures for compliance can be a force multiplier.

6. For additional commentary on the topic, please see my testimony at:
https://smallbusiness.house.gov/uploadedfiles/2-11-2016_wolf_testimony.pdf

Question

Mr. Mancuso, you noted that the Treasury's Office of Foreign Assets Control is "taking aggressive jurisdictional and interpretative positions" to bolster our sanctions regime against Iran. The *Export Control Reform Act* carries over important missile sanctions and chemical and biological weapons sanctions. Is the U.S. properly utilizing this sanctions authority to punish those who export dangerous items to rogue nations?

Answer

Last year, the *Countering America's Adversaries Through Sanctions Act* imposed new sanctions on Iran targeting its ballistic missile program. The U.S. Department of Commerce, Bureau of Industry and Security and the U.S. Department of the Treasury, Office of Foreign Assets Control have also been active in targeting individuals and entities supporting Iran's (and North Korea's) ballistic missile program. These efforts are essential to the U.S. government's broader strategy to counter Iran. While it appears that good work is currently being done in this regard, the pertinent provisions of the *Export Control Reform Act* would add another tool to address this urgent U.S. national security priority.

www.ingramcontent.com/pod-product-compliance
Lightning Source LLC
Chambersburg PA
CBHW080042260726
48658CB00007B/2701